All For You

By

EBONIA
(EB-BOW-NEE-AH)

Limousine Sketch by Darnell Gulley

1stBooks - rev. 01/24/03

Dedication

I dedicate this book, first and foremost to God because He gave me the talent to write.

To my mother Evangelist Elaine V. Ebo, who has been my supporter, my cheerleader, my motivator. To my dad, Rev. John H. Ebo because you taught me not to settle when I can do better. To my sons, Anthony, Nathaniel, Diallo, Jacob and William; I write because of you. To my brothers, Lonnie, Darien and John,Jr. because you buy my books no matter what's in them!

To Juanita and Roger, my favorite married couple and my very good friends. Thank you. To Dianna, who typed and typed and typed some more. I could not have done this without you. God bless your fingers. I will need your help again soon. To Julia, Ebba, Tamani, Jerry, Mahserg and Curtis, thank you all for lending me your ears. To Karen and Nneka, your great ideas have helped a lot.

Thank you and God bless you all.

Gabrielle Grayson is young, attractive and ambitious. She has just returned from a retreat that has given her new motivation on how to tap into her students learning potential. She has a good relationship with her mother and a boyfriend. Her life is far from perfect but she is content with things the way they are. Yet, a chance encounter with a handsome stranger changes the way she looks at love.

Anderson Ray, handsome, successful private investigator and a man on a mission to find his mother, the woman who gave him up when he was born. The only information he has was given to him by his father and his godfather. Anderson has questions, so many questions. Little does he realize that a good deed will provide the link he needs to get his questions answered.

CHAPTER I

When Gabrielle emerged from the chartered bus that pulled into Thirtieth Street Station in Philadelphia Saturday evening, she was sleepy and hungry. Even though the bus had arrived fifteen minutes early, she was not sure that Jimmy would pick her up as promised. She could not imagine what was keeping him. She told him that the bus would be pulling into the train station at six because some of the other people, who had attended the conference in upstate New York, were from New Jersey and Delaware. They would be taking trains home. About twenty Philadelphians from several small learning communities in the School District had attended the orientation. All of them, including Gabrielle had returned with new insight as to how to implement something called Service Learning into the school curriculum.

Gabrielle, her co-workers and some other teachers had been through eight grueling days of workshops and discussion groups at King's Cove, a gorgeous retreat in the mountains. The scenery had been breathtaking and the weather balmy but all Gabrielle wanted to do now, was go home. A few of her friends had helped her carry her luggage outside to the Twenty-ninth Street entrance and she had assured them that she would be fine.

While waiting for her boyfriend, she thought about the workshops. Many of the guest speakers there were instructors who already had their students doing projects as part of their regular schoolwork. Some of these youth were learning about the aging process and studying health issues while doing a community service for and sometimes with the elderly.

At another school, young people chose to focus on multiculturalism and were painting several murals to show the diversity of their neighborhoods while promoting harmony and respect among the residents.

1

Gabrielle could not help thinking that somebody was finally doing exactly what she felt needed to be done. She had always wondered what could be added to the students' classwork so they could have a more viable investment in the communities where they live and go to school. She had gotten her own idea but she did not know what to call it or how to put it in place. Service Learning was perfect and it enhanced their regular studies in some interesting ways.

Gabrielle had attended this conference at the urging of Ms. Parker, the third grade teacher at Moore Elementary School. Gabrielle was a Teaching Assistant in Ms. Parker's room. Since Ms. Parker could not go to the conference herself, she suggested that Gabrielle attend. They would meet later to discuss the workshops once Gabrielle returned.

She looked anxiously at her watch again. Eight o'clock. Gabrielle was starting to be concerned. She saw her co-workers being picked up one by one by family and friends and driving away. Some of her new acquaintances had already said their good-byes and left to board their trains. Someone even offered to give her a ride home but she knew that Jimmy would be angry if she left.

She had telephoned the apartment when she first arrived and there was no answer. Now, she was nowhere near a telephone and did not want to drag her luggage back into the building. Her denim outfit; the long split skirt, jacket and floppy hat were no longer comfortable. Even her T-shirt was sticking to her and her muscles ached.

She pulled out her latest issue of Essence Magazine and she looked up at the sky. It was getting dark quickly and on such a beautiful evening in June that could only mean one thing - Rain! The way the gray clouds were slowly drifting in, Gabrielle knew that the warm, sunny pre-summer day would fade into a cool, soggy night within the hour. She decided that the best thing to do was to push her luggage as close to the building as possible and try to squeeze under any overhang to stay dry. She had not packed an umbrella or any other rainwear but she had not anticipated waiting two hours or more to go home.

As she pushed the last piece of her designer luggage against the building, she heard thunder crack through the silence. It was so sudden it frightened her. The sound seemed to be amplified because the traffic around the train station had thinned to hardly any cars or taxis. Everyone seemed to be hustling to beat the rainfall. Everyone but Gabrielle.

Just as she sat down on the big Pullman suitcase and opened her magazine, lightning flashed across the sky. The wind picked up, so Gabrielle grabbed at her hat and pulled it more snugly on her head and put her magazine away.

"Terr-ri-fic," she muttered, looking at her watch again, "what else can go wrong?"

As if on cue, the sky opened up and rain poured down like sprinklers turning on full force.

"Oh no!" Gabrielle sighed as she dropped her head in surrender to Mother Nature. She was still looking down so she did the next logical thing that a twenty-four year old woman does in this predicament; she started to cry. She knew it was immature and she really did try to fight back the tears but she was tired and beginning to feel very abandoned.

Her head was down; her eyes welled up with tears so she did not see the off-white Excalibur Limousine pull up to the curb. She did not see the well-dressed man in the white dinner jacket get out with umbrella in hand and rush over to her. She did not really notice that the rain that had been falling so diligently on her hat was now silent. But when she heard the sonorous voice that could stop time - speak, Gabrielle thought she would faint.

"May I be of assistance?" said a voice every bit as deep as Barry White's.

Oh please, she thought, *please, don't let him be tall, dark and fine.* Before she looked up, she shut her eyes trying to convince herself that he was not everything she'd just imagined.

If she thought she was going to faint just hearing his voice, Gabrielle was sure she would buckle now. She opened her eyes as she raised her head and blinked in amazement. He was tall, even though she was sitting down, she knew he was tall. Since Gabrielle was five-eight, she guessed he had to be six-foot, maybe even six-two. He was well built with broad shoulders. He had close-cropped hair, cocoa-brown skin, a well-trimmed mustache and deep brown eyes to die for! He was no Denzel Washington, a popular actor of this day. He was more like the young Richard Roundtree. Gabrielle loved Richard Roundtree! From the first time her mother had rented the movie "Shaft" on videotape, Gabrielle had a huge crush. She watched the tape so many times, her mother teased her until she finally broke down and purchased the video for herself. Yet, this man standing before her even gave her favorite actor competition! She swallowed, trying to find her voice. *Oh great,* she thought, *and me looking like Raggedy Andy's sister!*

She was about to speak when a black BMW convertible came to a screeching halt and without even bothering to park properly, a young man dressed in black leather, got out leaving the driver's door open.

"S'matter, you couldn't wait?" the young driver yelled at her edging past the man with the umbrella. "I told you I'd be here. Why don't you listen when I tell you something? That's what's wrong with you. You never listen."

"Hello to you too, Jimmy," Gabrielle clipped back. "For your information, I have been waiting and waiting and…"

"So what's with Sir Galahad here?" Jimmy asked snidely as he pointed over his shoulder. He was now standing in front of the deep-voiced stranger.

"Anderson Ray," the Samaritan offered, closing his umbrella since the cloudburst had stopped.

"I wasn't talking to you," Jimmy said sharply. He did not even bother to turn around.

4

"That's true but you were referring to me so I thought I'd help you do it respectfully. You haven't been showing any so far," Anderson chastised.

Hearing that voice again, Gabrielle closed her eyes as if trying to absorb the sound. Jimmy saw her reaction and sucked his teeth. He turned to face Anderson in some strange macho stance. Anderson rose to his full height and stared at Jimmy, an intimidation move he had mastered long ago in his line of work. Success. Jimmy turned to direct his tirade at Gabrielle.

"Let's go, Gabby," he said through clenched teeth. He grabbed Gabrielle's left arm.

"Ow!" Gabrielle yelled pulling away from him. "What is your problem?"

Jimmy relaxed his grip but he did not let go of her. Gabrielle frowned at him and looked over his shoulder at Anderson who had stepped back to observe the whole scene.

He made no comment. Anderson had witnessed this scene numerous times. Being co-partner of Rayzor-Sharpe Security & Private Investigations, Inc., he had watched situations like this one unfold far too often. He took two steps back, poised himself and waited. He had a pretty good idea what would happen next.

Jimmy picked up one of Gabrielle's suitcases. "I said, 'Let's go.'" He raked the fingers of his right hand through his brown wavy hair. Then he growled, jerking her arm again.

"And I said, 'That hurts,'" Gabrielle said with a grimace. "Go yank on somebody else! Besides, I hate it when you call me 'Gabby'." She inched away from him, turned and grabbed her overnight bag.

"Shut up! And don't be tryin' ta front jus' 'cause of him," Jimmy warned, pointing a fisted thumb over his shoulder.

"You really should show the Sistah more respect," Anderson told him, stepping forward.

Releasing the suitcase, Jimmy turned to face him but at five feet-eight, his one hundred and seventy pounds paled next to Anderson who weighed two-thirty-five.

"So who are you, Miss Manners in drag?" Jimmy asked sarcastically.

"I'm somebody who knows how to treat a lady," Anderson told him matter-of-factly. Jimmy's jaw clenched and his right hand closed into a fist.

"She ain't no lady; she's a woman! And she's **my** woman at that; so why don't you just go play doorman somewhere."

Anderson frowned. Gabrielle shivered.

"Jimmy, we need to go," Gabrielle called trying to distract him. Jimmy turned. He was standing between Gabrielle and Anderson. Anderson was closer.

"Didn't I tell you to shut up? You 'bout one dumb—" Jimmy never finished. In the next moment, he found himself on his knees gasping for air.

"And I told **you** to show the Sistah more respect;" Anderson shook his head in disapproval. "You must not have gone on the March." Anderson was referring to the Million Man March to Washington, DC in October 1995.

"Some of us **really did** take the Pledge seriously."

He was now looking down at Jimmy. His hand had caught Jimmy's windpipe. He shook his wrist lightly and with the same hand, reached for the suitcase Jimmy had dropped.

He turned toward Gabrielle, gave her a slight bow and a warm smile.

"**Now**, may I be of assistance?" he asked, casting an eye toward Jimmy who was holding his throat, still struggling for air. Gabrielle looked too and gave Anderson a worried frown.

"He'll survive," he assured her, "but I can't do anything about his manners. They'll be just as bad tomorrow." Anderson reached in his black tuxedo pants pocket for his keypad. He unlocked the rear passenger door and the trunk of the limo.

Gabrielle stepped around Jimmy and Anderson guided her to the car. Once she was inside, he handed her the overnight bag and closed the door. Careful to keep a watchful eye on Jimmy, who had finally risen to his feet, Anderson loaded the rest of the luggage into the trunk, closed it and walked to the driver's side of the luxury car. He gave Jimmy one last frown as the younger man staggered toward his BMW.

Settling in the driver's seat, Anderson adjusted the rearview mirror to see his passenger more clearly.

"Where to?" he queried as Gabrielle looked around inside the gorgeous car. She had never seen anything like it, white leather interior, and black carpet on the floor. There was a stereo, miniature wet bar, small color TV with VCR, and what looked like a mini file cabinet with several small drawers. Gabrielle was curious but she did not dare touch anything.

Gabrielle looked up toward the mirror when he spoke and caught sight of those intense, brown eyes again. Something about those eyes told her that he could be trusted.

"521 Mt. Airy Circle."

His eyes narrowed just a bit as he looked at her. "That's not...?"

"Oh no, she answered quickly, reading his thoughts. "That's my mother's address."

His face relaxed and Anderson gave her that heart-stopping smile again.

"Okay. Now, why don't you sit back, relax and enjoy yourself." He put a Bill Withers CD in the player and LEAN ON ME eased through the speakers as Anderson started the car.

He looked up to see Gabrielle's eyes close and her head ease back against the seat. He saw her shoulders droop slightly and she moved her head from side to side as if trying to relieve tension. He could tell she was tired and it certainly did not take a rocket scientist to figure out that this tired was not just due to today's events. This tired had been mounting for a long, long time.

Gabrielle allowed herself to get comfortable and looked around. *No one would ever believe this*, she thought. *In fact, I'm not sure I believe it myself.* She could not remember the last time someone had treated her like she was special. Jimmy certainly didn't and hadn't in quite a while. *What was it Mr. Ray had said? "Respect the Sistah."* Yes, it had been a while since a man made her feel like this. As she closed her eyes, she took in the words of the song coming through the speakers and thought it was an interesting choice or maybe, it really was just a coincidence.

Anderson eased the big car toward Market Street and headed for downtown Center City. He could have taken the Expressway but decided to allow his attractive guest to enjoy a longer ride. He drove to Twentieth Street and took the Parkway to West River Drive. He checked the clock on the dashboard. It was almost nine o'clock. He would have her to her destination in about an hour.

As he guided the Excalibur in and out of traffic, he glanced in the rearview mirror at his passenger. Her shoulder length braids were twisted into a curly style framing her almond-shaped face. Her caramel brown skin had a warm, natural shine as if someone had bathed her in baby oil. When he had touched her hand as she got in the car, it had a baby smooth feel. He was also pleased with the fact that she was not skinny. Anderson did not find skinny women especially appealing. Gabrielle was shapely. A woman of substance is what he'd call her. He was so busy in his own thoughts that he did not hear the low voice that called his name.

"Excuse me, Mr. Ray? Uh, Mr. Ray?" Her sweet, smooth voice broke into his thoughts.

"Anderson," he corrected gently.

"Okay…An-der-son." She said his name slowly. It sounded like music as it tickled his ear. He looked up into the mirror. Gabrielle had found the intercom. The car was also equipped with a phone for more private conversations between passenger and driver.

"Won't your boss be upset if you don't pick him up on time?" she asked with genuine concern.

Anderson caught himself before he laughed out loud and merely smiled. *That's cute*, he thought. *She thinks I'm the chauffeur. No, my dear, he won't be upset in the least. This is my car. On the odd chance we get to speak again, I might even*

8

get to explain that to you. But there's certainly no hurry on that one. Besides, if we never cross paths again, it doesn't really matter.

"Uh, Mr. Ray...I mean, Anderson?"

Anderson noted that she was still waiting for an answer. "Hmmm? Oh, I'm sorry, Miss...?"

"Gabrielle."

"Gabrielle." He didn't say it. He breathed it. It came out mellow and sexy and went all the way down her spine.

Unconsciously, Gabrielle let a sigh slip from her lips. She had slipped off her shoes when she got in the car. Now, she wriggled her toes in the plush carpet to distract herself. Anderson smiled. He knew what his voice did to women. Even though he seldom used it to manipulate them, he was pleased with the effect it was having on this one.

"Not to worry, M'Lady," he replied softly, "I have the car for the night. You just relax. For now, this is your limousine and I...am at your service." Not knowing what to say, Gabrielle slid back on the seat and rested her head on the soft leather.

Anderson changed the music to a Phyllis Hyman CD and adjusted the speakers so that Phyllis's voice floated all through the car. Soon Gabrielle was so relaxed she drifted off to sleep. This time, Anderson popped in the jazz sounds of Gato Barbieri and went into another zone himself.

He maneuvered the sleek, luxury car along West River Drive. He had given Nate, his chauffeur and bodyguard, the day off and because of a special meeting; he opted to drive the big car instead of his black Pathfinder or his silver-gray Cadillac sedan. Other than those, his favorite was this creme, off-white and brass limousine. This long, elegant, custom designed, one-of-a-kind car; painted the color of mother-of-pearl, was his baby. He relished the times when he did not have to do the driving but he was especially fond of the occasions when he and Nate would drive through their old neighborhoods.

Often, they would pull up to the curb and see young children staring in awe at such a big unique looking car and their surprise

9

increased when they saw a Black man get out of the back seat for a change. Nate and Anderson would talk to those boys and girls about how someday they too, could be in the same kind of car. They would tell them that they don't have to sell drugs to gain wealth and respect. They also told them that even though there might be nothing wrong with trying to be "like Mike," they had people in their own neighborhoods they should admire, imitate and emulate. That would usually start a whole new line of questions.

Anderson came by his fondness of cars honestly. His grandfather, Harrison Ray raised him, after a drunk driver killed his father when Anderson was a little boy. His grandfather was afraid Anderson would grow up with a fear or a dislike of cars as a result of the accident, so he taught the boy everything he knew about automobiles. They eventually built a car together, Anderson's cherry-red Mercury Cougar that he still kept in top running condition.

His grandfather had taught him to respect these "machines of motion" as he called them. "Andy," he'd say, "treat your car with respect. It will carry very important cargo every day - You! Never abuse the privilege to drive and watch out for the fools."

"Fools!" Anderson said out loud. *Like Jimmy*, he mused, remembering how the young man had careened to a halt, leaving his door open when he got out of the car. *That's the same kind of recklessness that killed my dad.* He gripped the steering wheel tighter. He glanced back at Gabrielle who had stretched out on the seat in a deep sleep. The split in her skirt had shifted so more of her leg was showing just above the knee. It was beautiful, like the rest of her. How the devil did someone so sweet get tangled up with a hothead like Jimmy? And for that matter…why did he care?

He brought his attention back to the road just in time to apply the brakes and avoid an accident. Another car had darted into his lane much too close without signaling. He stopped in time but the car jerked slightly. He relaxed his grip on the wheel and checked in the mirror. Gabrielle had not stirred. That's exactly why he loved this car!

The recklessness of the other driver took Anderson's thoughts back to his father. Clayton Ray had been eighteen and had just graduated high school when he found out he was going to be a father. His girlfriend, Anderson's mother, saw the whole thing as an inconvenience and wanted an abortion but Clayton was raised to not run away from his responsibility. He begged her to have the baby. Since she did not want to stay with him, Clayton took custody and with the help of his father, raised his son as a single dad.

It had been hard not to be bitter when his grandfather told him about the accident that wasn't really an accident. The driver, who had been going much too fast, had fled the scene and it was a long time before Anderson's injured father was spotted by another driver. Even though paramedics were called and Clayton Ray was taken to the hospital, his internal injuries had been serious. Anderson learned later that if his father had arrived at the hospital sooner, he might have had a chance. Anderson saw the whole thing as the senseless act of a callous person and he had a difficult time handling the tragedy. He became an angry five-year-old after his father died and he had a lot of resentment building in him as he grew up. That resentment toward those who broke the law was what helped him decide to become a police officer. For several years, he worked diligently, arresting those who broke the law and it frustrated him whenever guys like Jimmy ignored it.

He brought his concentration back to the present. Listening to the music, as he watched the road, Anderson let Jimmy quickly become less of a factor in the evening's events.

CHAPTER II

Brandeis Grayson often glanced out of her window on cool nights especially after a flash storm. The air always smelled crisp and for a second or two everything was washed clean. Nothing had prepared her for the scene taking place before her eyes at ten o'clock this June evening.

When Mrs. Grayson saw the long white limo pull up in front of her house, she figured someone was lost and needed directions. When she saw the tall, good-looking man get out of the car, she didn't care what they needed. *Just let me look at him a little while longer*, she thought. But when she saw her daughter being helped from the back seat by the same man, she thought God had finally smiled on her prayers.

"Mercy me," she cried checking her make-up and jet black hair in the mirror near her vestibule, "My baby done gone and did something right! Thank you, Lord." She ran to the door, opening it and her arms to her daughter. Anderson followed, his arms full with three pieces of luggage. Gabrielle greeted her mother with a half-smile when she hugged her.

"I know that look," her mother stated, "What did Fool do this time?" She eyed Anderson out of the corner of her eye as she placed a comforting arm around her daughter's waist since Gabrielle stood a good six inches taller than her mother. Over her shoulder, she indicated where Anderson could put the bags down and walked with her daughter in tow to the living room.

"Mother, I wish you wouldn't call him that. His name's Jimmy."

"His name's Fool if he hurt my baby," Mrs. Grayson said emphatically. "And he must have done something really stupid if this magnificent creature brought you home."

"Mom!" Gabrielle yelled as her cheeks flushed.

Anderson had set the suitcases in the hallway and followed them into the room.

"Don't you 'Mom' me, I call 'em as I see 'em." She told her daughter. "He's darling and by the smile on his face, I'll bet I'm not the first red-blooded woman to notice." Mrs. Grayson turned her attention to the stranger who filled up her doorway.

"The name's Anderson Ray and I'm not sure if you'd win the bet, but I do thank you for the compliment," he told her as he flashed a smile and stepped forward. She smiled back looking him up and down and nodding.

"All that and the voice of thunder too!" Brandeis teased, patting her chest rapidly. "Mercy! Wherever did Gigi find you?" Anderson chortled as she gave him a once-over with her eyes and smiled. "Hi, I'm Brandeis Grayson," she said offering Anderson her hand.

He had taken note of the endearment used by Gabrielle's mother earlier and decided it suited Gabrielle perfectly. Anderson shook Mrs. Grayson's hand and looked at Gabrielle who quickly broke into their exchange.

"Mr. Ray, uh…I mean, Anderson was nice enough to give me a ride from the station when Jimmy and I had a difference of opinion."

"As if he **ever** had an opinion that was worth anything," Brandeis quipped. Anderson snickered and Gabrielle rolled her eyes.

"Mom, I wish you wouldn't be so hard on him and please, not in front of strangers."

"Oh hush, Gigi. This man ain't a stranger. He's a guardian angel," Brandeis said. Her last remark was made with a voice that could have been used to advertise cologne.

Once again, Brandeis smiled at Anderson who responded with one of his lopsided grins before turning to leave. Gabrielle walked him to the door.

"Thank you for bringing my baby to me safe and sound," Brandeis called after him.

Anderson turned to look at Gabrielle's mother; he gave a slight bow.

"I assure you, Mrs. Grayson, it was my pleasure." With that, he pivoted and walked to the door. Brandeis laughed and shook her head. *Good looking, confident, takes a compliment in stride and isn't full of himself. Watch out, Gigi,* she thought, *this one's smooth as silk. And I approve.*

"Thanks for...for what you did back there and for bringing me here," Gabrielle told him without looking up.

After Anderson opened the door, he turned to Gabrielle. "Gigi, huh?" he spoke her nickname with a softer "g" sound; not the hard way her mother said it. He made it sound French and sensual. Gabrielle shivered. She dropped her eyes and looked at the floor. Anderson put his thumb and index finger under her chin and lifted her head. She sure was pretty when she blushed.

"It was all for you," he told her. "You deserve to be treated like somebody special." He looked into her eyes for what felt like a long moment and in a voice barely above a whisper he said, "Stay safe." When he drove away, Gabrielle was still standing in the doorway.

"Mother, how could you?" Gabrielle asked confronting her mother as she walked back into the house. "That was absolutely shameful."

"Now you watch your tone with me, Sister-girl. When did honesty become shameful? Besides, have you ever known me to not speak my mind? I will not apologize for who I am. He was a sight for sore eyes if ever I saw one. Baby, when I saw you get out of that fabulous car, well, I thought finally..."

"It doesn't matter what you thought," Gabrielle broke in, "and anyway, he's a chauffeur."

Brandeis hooted. "Oh please, Gigi. Were we looking at the same person? You must be blind. A man with that much style and finesse; he doesn't work for people, Sugar, they work for him!"

Gabrielle was about to debate her mother's last comment when she heard a car pull up outside. She thought Anderson had forgotten to leave something. Doing a quick count of her luggage, she realized it had to be something else. She hurried to the door but she stopped short of opening it when she saw Jimmy standing on the porch.

Jimmy spotted her through the front door's window but when she did not open the door for him, he became agitated. He grabbed at the screen door's handle, finding it locked, he swore violently.

"Are you gonna open this door or what?" he yelled. "I ain't got all night. Let's go."

Gabrielle's mother had been sitting on the sofa when she got an eerie feeling and the hairs on the back of her neck tingled. As she walked toward her door, she was not surprised when she heard Jimmy's loud voice yelling at her daughter.

"What the devil do **you** want?" she asked.

"Don't start with me, woman. I came for Gabby and then I'm out…"

"Her name is Gabrielle and you're out now or aren't you looking?" Brandeis shot back. "My daughter goes nowhere with you tonight. If I had anything to say about it, she'd go nowhere with you anymore."

"Like you said, 'if you had anything to say about it,' but you don't, so back off," Jimmy railed.

"Why you arrogant…"

"Mom please, I'll handle this," Gabrielle told her. Turning her attention to Jimmy, she narrowed her eyes. Keeping both doors locked between them, she looked at him through the window.

"Jimmy, pay attention, you do not; I repeat **do not**, own me and I am not going anywhere with you tonight. And if your attitude hasn't changed by tomorrow, I'll stay here tomorrow, too."

"Amen!" Brandeis injected folding her arms while standing next to her daughter. Jimmy glared at her then turned his attention to Gabrielle.

15

"Who do you think you're talkin' to?" Jimmy asked fuming. "You think just because some dude in a fancy car pays you some attention, you can dis me? You either get out here and in the car or I'll leave you here and I do mean leave you here!"

Jimmy walked to the end of the porch and waited, sure that Gabrielle would come out and go with him. When she did not, he walked back to the door. Looking through the door, he only saw Brandeis. Gabrielle had walked back into the living room.

"What did you think, Fool, 'cause you said 'frog' she was gonna ask, 'how high?' My daughter is much smarter than that and I pray to God that she has really come to her senses," Brandeis told him calmly.

"Yeah. So you say. I know you ain't never liked me anyway and now, you got Gabby all confused about..."

"Confused?" Brandeis broke in. "Today, she finally got a taste of how a real man treats a woman and I hope it woke her up. Jimmy, you know what your problem is? You're stuck on stupid and broke down on dumb! You've got a good woman, Jimmy and you treat her so bad you deserve what you get."

Jimmy balled up his fist and raised it toward the window.

"See, that's what I mean. That's your answer to everything, isn't it, Jimmy? You're a hothead and that will get you in more trouble than anything else." Brandeis suddenly softened her tone. She wanted to get through to him for once. "Look, James, when Gabrielle first brought you by the house, I thought, what a nice young man. So nice looking and you were quite a charmer. But then, a few months later, when the two of you started dating regularly, you changed. You got bossy and possessive and I **know** you been hittin' my baby. I lost all respect for you then and I will never treat you like a man until you act like one."

"A real man does not hit a woman, Jimmy. A real man knows how to walk away. Even if she provokes him, he will still walk away."

Jimmy started to deny her allegation but Brandeis held up her hand.

"Don't bother, Jimmy, I've heard most of the excuses. I know you've threatened her and you've verbally abused her many times. You put bruises on the one person I cherish. If you were smart, you'd cherish her too, but you don't have that much sense. If you don't get it together, you will lose her. Do you hear me, son?"

"I **ain't** your son," Jimmy snarled.

"That's the first correct thing you've said standing here," Brandeis snapped, her anger and frustration rising again. "You are not my son and I hope and pray you will never be my son-in-law!"

Suddenly, Gabrielle appeared in the vestibule and shouted at her mother. "Mom, what are you doing? You can't talk to him like that."

Jimmy curled his lip as his face took on a smug expression and Brandeis turned to her daughter and her eyes widened. "Say what?" She could not believe her ears.

"Mom, I've asked you not to treat…"

"Oh, not again, Sister-Girl. Every time you do this, you go right back…"

"Well, so what…?" Gabrielle answered defensively. "Jimmy and I live together and if you can't accept that…"

"Accept it? Accept it? Not as long as he **beats** on you. If I've told you once, I've said it a million times; you deserve better. And you will keep hearing it from me until you find better."

Brandeis reached up and touched her daughter's cheek. "Baby, I love you. He doesn't," Brandeis added pointing to Jimmy through the door. "Love hurts sometimes, Baby, I know that but love is **not** violent."

Brandeis closed her eyes to hide the tears that were ready to fall at any minute. When she opened them, Gabrielle already had some of her luggage near the door. Sad eyes were exchanged between mother and daughter. Realizing that her protests would not do any good, Brandeis stepped aside.

Gabrielle opened the door and Jimmy reached in and grabbed the bags as Gabrielle pushed them through the doorway. Brandeis folded her arms across her chest and looked away. Once all the luggage was on the porch, Gabrielle looked back at her mother. She took the three steps that separated them and spoke.

"Mom, you just don't understand."

Brandeis looked at her daughter. There was love and sympathy in her eyes. She choked back a sob as she touched her cheek again. "You got that right. I don't and I won't **ever**, not this." She paused before she continued, "but I love you, Gigi. You can always come back here. You will always find..."

"I know, Ma-Dear," Gabrielle interrupted using her own term of endearment from childhood. Gabrielle had put her finger to her mother's lips and then she leaned down and hugged her tight. Brandeis hugged back even tighter hoping her daughter would draw strength from her. With a small voice she whispered in her daughter's ear, "Be safe, Gigi. Please be safe." Gabrielle remembered it was almost the same thing Anderson had said.

Brandeis stood in the doorway a long time after Jimmy and her daughter drove away. She closed the door with a tear in her eye. As she walked back in the living room, she shivered. No one had to tell her what would happen the moment this couple reached their apartment. Brandeis hugged herself tight and went to the window. Peering up into the night sky, she tried to blink back new tears.

"Please God," she prayed, "if it's gonna happen, don't let it be too bad this time. I just wish You'd fix things so it wouldn't happen any more!"

CHAPTER III

The moment Jimmy had set the bags inside their second floor apartment he turned on Gabrielle with fire in his eyes. Gabrielle still had her overnight bag in her hand. She had been walking behind Jimmy and since he had been silent the whole ride home, she thought he was no longer angry. She set her bag next to the ones Jimmy had put in the living room near their black leather loveseat and barely had time to straighten up before he grabbed her roughly by the same arm that was already sore.

They were toe to toe when she smelled it. He'd been drinking. She hadn't smelled any liquor earlier at the train station. No doubt after that scene, he had gone to drown his wounded pride. He wasn't drunk but he was spoiling for a fight. Gabrielle backed up but Jimmy did not release her.

"Just what did you think you were doing today, Gabby Girl?"

"Oww! Jimmy, I told you that hurt."

"Does it really?" he asked, his lips dripping with sarcasm. "Do you have any idea how much pain you caused me? You made me look bad today Sistah, very, very bad."

He tightened his grip and dragged her to the sofa. He shoved her down. Since they were just about the same height, he always pushed her down when he wanted to overpower her.

Gabrielle was in pain and afraid. Jimmy had been embarrassed and she knew that whenever he felt belittled, he had to assert his manhood that much more. She usually caught the brunt of it when he did, especially when he tried to soothe his ego with liquor first.

"Jimmy," Gabrielle began, "you brought a lot of what happened to you today on yourself. I told you that I don't like it when you disrespect me. I told you…"

"You told me? You told me? Get this straight, Sistah, you don't **tell me** nothing! You ain't my mother!" Jimmy shoved her again and stood over her.

19

"Jimmy, this isn't about being your mother. This is about us and how you treat me." Gabrielle explained when the pain in her arm had eased so she could speak.

"I treat you just fine," Jimmy retorted, "besides, if you didn't like it you could have stayed at your mom's."

Gabrielle winced at the truth in those words and shut her eyes. Finally, she tried pleading with him.

"Jimmy, please don't do this. I just got back from a conference and I'm tired. We don't have to fight."

"Oh, you are so-o-o right," he sneered, "why fight? There are other things we could be doing."

The tone in his voice made Gabrielle tremble. When she looked into his eyes she wanted to run and hide. She tried again to get him to listen to reason.

"Jimmy, not tonight, okay? I'm tired and after everything that's happened, I've got a headache."

Oh no you don't. I'm not fallin' for that 'I've got a headache' lie. What do you take me for?"

"Jimmy, please. It's not a lie. All I want is…"

"Oh, I know what you want, Sistah. That's what I want too," Jimmy answered ignoring the desperation in her voice while tugging at her clothes. Gabrielle's eyes widened as she realized his intentions.

"It's been days and I need to know that you missed me." His eyes were slits now under an evil frown. His menacing tone sent a chill up Gabrielle's spine.

"Besides," he continued, "you have to make up for how I was treated today. You dissed me in front of your mom and that guy. That was so wrong, Baby, oh so wrong. Now, you're gonna make up for it. Do you hear me?"

Jimmy was like a mad man. Even though Gabrielle repeatedly begged him to wait until she had gotten some rest or at least took a bath, he grabbed her by her braids and hauled her in the bedroom and violently kicked the door closed. For the next two hours, the neighbors heard a woman's crying and a man's yelling coming from that apartment.

At about one o'clock in the morning, Brandeis sat straight up in her bed. She had that tingling sensation on the back of her neck again. Tears of frustration began to ease down her cheeks.

"Oh God, she moaned, "I know you said 'Vengeance is Mine' but..." She did not finish, instead, she grabbed her Bible from the nightstand and began reading the Twenty-Third Psalm. After reading it through once, Brandeis began again, changing it to third person speech. "The Lord is her Shepherd; she shall not want. He maketh her to lie down in green pastures. He leadeth her beside the still waters. He restoreth her soul." When she finished reading this time; she turned to Psalm 91 and read until she fell asleep again.

Jimmy abused and berated Gabrielle all weekend. He did not allow her to go anywhere without him. He was so cruel that she was emotionally and physically exhausted. She was grateful whenever sleep overtook her.

Monday, when Gabrielle awoke, it was about eight o'clock in the morning. Her entire body was sore. Her neck and arms were bruised. Jimmy had been merciless all weekend. The night she came home, he had not let her fall asleep until five the next morning. He had been rough in the past but this time he was even meaner. Gabrielle suspected it had something to do with Anderson being on the scene Saturday. As she struggled to roll over, Gabrielle was grateful that Jimmy had left early.

She picked up the phone and called the school to tell them she was taking a sick day. She had earned the time. She needed to take it. She did not want anyone to see her today, especially the children in her class. She told the secretary that she would probably be in the next day. Then she dragged herself into the bathroom to soak in a tub she filled with mineral salts.

Gabrielle was so exhausted and stressed she fell asleep in the tub. The ringing of the telephone woke her with a start and she suddenly felt a chill because the water had gotten cold. She hurriedly got out of the tub, grabbed a towel and ran to answer the phone.

"Gigi, are you all right?" Her mother asked as soon as she heard Gabrielle's voice.

"Yes Mom, I'm fine," she answered as she wrapped the towel around herself. "Why do you ask?" It was a moot question. Gabrielle knew why. They had replayed this conversation many times in the last six months.

"Gigi!" Brandeis spoke more intensely. "**Are you** all right? When I didn't hear from you Sunday, I was worried." Brandeis gripped the receiver tightly. She swallowed hard while she waited. This time, Gabrielle did not answer right away.

"Oh, Baby. No-o-o." Brandeis sobbed and Gabrielle let out the breath that was holding back the tears she was trying to conceal. Mother and daughter were crying now, each one for different reasons but both were in pain.

"It's okay, Baby, I'm not going to lecture but I wish you would reconsider and come back home."

"Mom, I **am** home," Gabrielle argued weakly. "Jimmy was just upset over seeing me with another man and even though nothing happened, he thought…"

"Gigi, do you think I give a knat's behind what he thought?" Brandeis cut in. "Do you think I am the least bit concerned about that fool? When will you realize…?" Her mother stopped when she became aware that she was about to start an old familiar speech for the umpteenth time.

"Honey," Brandeis said carefully, changing the subject, along with her tone, "I have an idea. Why don't you come over today? We can have lunch and you can tell me all about your trip."

"I'm sorry, Mom. Maybe some other time. I want to straighten up the apartment, cook Jimmy a nice dinner and be here when he gets home."

Brandeis sucked her teeth. "What am I hearing? You mean to tell me that he couldn't even keep the place nice while you were gone? You just got back from a trip for God sake! Did he leave a mess for you to clean up?" Brandeis was angry and her frustration was mounting. She didn't even wait for her daughter to answer. She decided to end the conversation before she got even angrier. With a very low and somber "I love you," she hung up the phone.

Brandeis picked up the thick, yellow telephone book with both hands and threw it to the floor shouting, "Father, give me strength!" She sat down in the chair at the little desk in her dining room. Her hands shook and she was breathing hard.

"God," she cried, "did I do this to my daughter? I walked away from that man the **first** time he hit me. Did I not leave soon enough for her to understand?"

Brandeis sobbed heavily with her head in her hands. She put her head down on the desk and cried. After a few minutes, she composed herself and decided the best thing to do was to work in her garden. She went in the kitchen to her little corner sink and got her gardening tools. She decided to transplant the rose bushes she'd bought earlier in the month. She had put it off hoping that she would do this task with her daughter. They spent a lot of quality time together working in her garden but now, she needed something to do. She wanted to clear her mind of evil thoughts; things that she knew she shouldn't wish on Jimmy.

CHAPTER IV

Since hers was a corner house, Brandeis could usually see cars as they turned into her block. Even from her backyard she had a clear view of the intersections of Mandela Drive and Mt. Airy Circle. It would have been hard to miss the pearl-white limo that turned onto her street.

"Oh my goodness," she exclaimed as she got up from her knees and hurried into the house. She washed her hands and quickly turned on the kettle so she could offer a cup of coffee or tea. She grabbed a paper towel. Wiping the sweat from her forehead, she turned off the burner and grabbed two glasses instead. She decided iced tea or lemonade would be better. After she put ice in the glasses, she waited just in case her eyes had deceived her. Her doorbell rang five minutes later.

"Good morning, Mrs. Grayson." Anderson, dressed in a tan, two-piece khaki set, greeted her with a smile when she opened the door.

After he entered the house, Brandeis caught sight of another man, casually leaning against the limousine. She could not see his face because he seemed to be looking at his shoes. Yet, he fascinated her and she had no idea why. She became very aware of a strange sensation at the back of her neck.

The man was wearing a short sleeved, charcoal gray shirt with matching pants, black shoes and driving gloves. He sported the typical chauffeur's cap. When he looked up, she noticed he was wearing a pair of Luxottica sunglasses, which gave him a mysterious look. He looked up and saw Brandeis in her doorway. He tipped his cap slightly and dropped his eyes again. Brandeis turned her attention to her guest. She gave Anderson a questioning look.

"That's my partner, Nathan Sharpe. For now, he wants to wait outside while we talk."

Brandeis shrugged and gestured toward the living room. Anderson stepped back and indicated that she should go first.

It was a cozy room. Anderson had noticed that Saturday night; cozy but rich with color. The walls were a pale peach. The woodwork in the room was natural with just enough stain to give it luster. The entrance from the vestibule divided the first wall. There was an abundant amount of African-American art and African artifacts framing the doorway. The second wall, behind the sofa held the big picture window and on either side of it was an array of awards received by mother or daughter for various achievements. The last wall had a fireplace and a mantle full of photos; Gabrielle's various graduation pictures and a few pictures of Brandeis.

The room was furnished with a number of pieces of wicker furniture, some natural hardwood chairs with colorful pillows and a brown corduroy loveseat and chair. There were several pieces of kente cloth prints draped on some of the chairs. This room did indeed have the Brandeis touch!

Anderson sat on the loveseat and Brandeis took her favorite seat, the high-back wicker rocking chair. She wore her hair short, in a natural cut and it framed her face like a crown. Wearing her turquoise caftan she looked like an African queen.

"So, what brings a busy man like you to my doorstep?" Brandeis asked.

"I was concerned about Gabrielle, Mrs. Grayson. I'm guessing that after I left, Jimmy showed up and I'm sure the scene was not pretty. Being a private investigator, I've witnessed too many incidents like what happened at the train station on Saturday and I've seen worse. I hope your daughter is all right. She left with him didn't she?"

Anderson stopped talking when he saw Brandeis clench her hands several times. He noticed that her face had a pained expression. He didn't miss much these days. One of the things he learned to read well was body language. Sometimes people said more when they were not speaking. Brandeis shifted position several times and was struggling hard to hold her emotions together. She dropped her eyes more than once. Each time she looked up at Anderson, she tried to speak but the words got stuck in her throat. She rose from her seat and went to the picture window.

Seeing the man, who was still leaning against the limo, triggered something and Brandeis began to sob. It was really more like a whimper. Ordinarily, no one would have heard it. No one but Anderson. Years of training taught him to notice the most minute sounds, the most insignificant gestures. Sometimes, he wondered if being good at his job was a curse.

He came and stood behind her. He did not touch her but he knew that she knew he was there if she needed him. He wanted her to know that she could trust him. He knew she was struggling to hold herself in check. He respected that. Once again, he waited.

"He abuses her, you know," she began slowly while continuing to look out the window. She focused her gaze on the man outside, the big man leaning against the limo. He had looked up again, toward her.

"He grabs her, shoves her around. Once, he pulled her braids so hard..." Her voice wavered for a minute. The man by the limo was still looking in her direction.

She was not sure if he could see her clearly. She knew he could not hear what she was saying but somehow, she was drawing strength from him. "I nearly lost it when she left again with that...that Fool!"

Anderson touched her elbow lightly and she moved away from the window. He led her to the dining room so she could sit at the table. He wanted her to have something to lean on. In his office, when clients were upset, he made sure they could lean on his desk. Brandeis rested her arms on the table and Anderson took the seat to the left at the head of the table so he could see her. Her gaze dropped again and her hands trembled.

"I don't know what to do for my baby. Sometimes, I feel so helpless. I mean, I know she's grown and it's her life but...Oh, why am I telling you this? I don't mean to burden you with..." She seemed to be talking more for herself than to him. Anderson touched her hand and she looked into his eyes. His gaze was patient, encouraging.

"She keeps telling me she knows what she's doing but I swear, I don't think she does. I just don't believe she does."

Brandeis did let the tears flow this time. Anderson squeezed the hand he was holding and at the same time, he handed her a handkerchief. When she raised her head, Anderson was looking into the green-gray eyes of a pleading mother. She'd tugged at his heart and Gabrielle already intrigued him. He wanted to help but he was not sure what he could do. He had handled enough abuse cases when he was on the police force to last a lifetime. He knew how difficult they could be. One minute, the guy is on his way to jail. The next minute, he's out because his woman has paid his bail money or worse, she decided not to press charges. In some instances, that decision proved fatal later when she was removed from the house in a body bag.

Yes, in seven years, he had had his fill of it so, he went back to school and then into private investigation. Even in this line of work, he still dealt with a few cases of abuse; a husband enraged when he finds out the wife has been cheating...a father who can't handle the fact that his daughter is getting older and turning into a woman...the list goes on. His thoughts were interrupted by a knock at the door.

"Sorry to disturb you, Air, but I'm gonna take a walk around the block. I just wanted you to know 'cause I'm leaving the limo."

"Yeah sure, Nate, that's fine. I shouldn't be too much longer." Anderson nodded to his friend and mentor. This man had taught him a lot of what he knew about their business; mainly the part that was not taught in the classroom. *Always the security man*, Anderson thought. *He's not fooling me. He's going to peruse the perimeter.*

He closed the screen door but since it was a nice day, Anderson left the front door open. A gentle breeze drifted in and Anderson took a deep breath. When he went back to the dining room, Brandeis was entering from the kitchen with a tray and three glasses of lemonade.

"I thought you might like some lemonade," she told him as he entered the room. Brandeis looked past him toward the doorway. Her anxious look turned into a frown. Anderson smiled.

"I promise I'll introduce you as soon as he comes back," Anderson teased. Her eyes widened and then she went into full denial.

"I swear, Anderson, I don't know what you're talking about," she declared in feigned innocence. Then they both laughed. They sat at the table again and he took her hand.

"It's good to see you laugh," he told her. Then in a more serious tone, he added, "Mrs. Grayson, I want you to know that I appreciate you confiding in me. I won't do anything to violate that trust. I do want to help. I don't know what I can do but I promise I will help."

"I knew you were a good man when I first saw you. I just wish my baby had met...OOPS! That's a mother talking too much again. I appreciate you letting me sound off about..."

There was another knock at the door.

When Brandeis entered the vestibule to answer the door, she was awestruck! Nathan Sharpe was truly a big man! His shoulders filled her doorway more than Anderson's had earlier. She took a step back and struggled to breathe.

"It's open," she called through the door after swallowing the lump in her throat. Nathan opened the door and stepped inside. As he was walking, he removed his cap and sunglasses. Brandeis looked up and saw a perfectly shaped bald head. *Have Mercy! If "Mr. T." had a brother without a Mohawk...he'd be standing in my house right now!* she thought.

The more Nathan stepped forward, the more Brandeis backed up. They both stopped walking abruptly and they were practically in the dining room. They just stood there staring at each other. Neither one said a word.

Anderson covered the grin on his face and cleared his throat. No one heard him. He did it again. Nathan looked at him but Brandeis just blushed. Nathan turned back in time enough to see her face and smiled a broad smile that revealed his deep dimples hiding between his smooth black beard and mustache.

"Oh my God!" she exclaimed as she did a quick intake of breath and her mouth flew open. Anderson snorted. Nathan frowned at him and turned back to Brandeis.

"Brandeis Grayson, this is my partner, Nathan Sharpe," Anderson said trying to keep the amusement out of his voice and the grin from his face. He was fascinated with Brandeis's reaction to his mentor. She was absolutely mesmerized. And something was happening to Nathan too.

"I am very happy to meet you, Mrs. Grayson. It is not often that my eyes grace such an elegant sight so early in the day." Nathan took her hand and even though she had offered it palm down, turned it over and kissed her fingertips. Brandeis sighed out loud, snatching her hand back as if something had burned it.

Anderson was holding his side and grinning. He went in the dining room to keep from breaking out in gales of laughter in front of them.

When Brandeis heard Nathan's voice, it had taken her breath away. It was not deep and rich like Anderson's. It was husky and full of whispers. It floated from between his lips like a baritone melody and Brandeis was having a hard time concentrating. She cleared her throat in an effort to get her voice back. She was still admiring his cinnamon brown complexion and suddenly asked, "I'll bet when you were in school, you could not escape a nickname. So, what on earth did they call you?" Brandeis asked trying to make light conversation.

"Copper Penny!' Oh man, did that ever burn me up." Nathan answered as his face flushed with excitement. "My skin

29

color has been either a curse…or an asset. It usually depends on the circumstances."

"So tell me," Brandeis said trying to distract herself away from his baldhead. "Who in your family is Native American?" She was looking at his high cheekbones and little-boy round face. Except for the gray in his beard, he could have passed for a man the same age as Anderson.

"My Nana…I mean, my paternal grandmother. She was Blackfoot. She died a few years ago," Nathan added solemnly. Brandeis gave him a nod of understanding and by mutual unspoken agreement they changed the subject to something lighter.

As he listened from the dining room, Anderson was pleased that his friend had lifted this lady's mood. He grabbed the tray with the glasses of lemonade. By the time he came into the living room, Nathan and Brandeis were discussing the artwork on her living room walls. As they stood side by side, it was hard not to conjure up the old Mutt and Jeff jokes that came to mind as Anderson observed them. Nathan's six-foot frame towered over Brandeis, who stood only five-two but he seemed comfortable with her and listened to her every word intently. When they noticed Anderson, they went to sit down. This time, when Brandeis took the rocking chair, Nathan took the hardwood seat right next to her. Anderson sat on the loveseat again, across from them.

"Fifty!" Brandeis said suddenly looking at Nathan.

"Ow, that's pretty good," Nathan answered with a grin, "but I'm forty-eight." There was a short pause. Nathan rubbed his chin and then smiled.

"Thirty!" Nathan shot back smugly.

"Why you wonderful man!" Brandeis purred as she smiled at him and touched his arm. Everybody laughed but Brandeis still did not tell him she was forty-three. *Maybe later*, she thought, admiring those dimples again.

The three of them visited for a little while longer just holding casual conversation and getting to know each other. Brandeis eventually told them that Gabrielle was a teacher's assistant at Moore Elementary School while studying English and Journalism at Community College. She also mentioned to them that Gabrielle had recruited her to participate in Career Month at the school. She would be going in Tuesday or Wednesday this week. She also suggested that more participants would probably be welcome. The men smiled at her not so subtle hint.

They said their good-byes about noon and Anderson and Nathan waved to Brandeis who stood in her doorway until they drove off. Anderson had taken the rear passenger seat when he got into the limousine. He picked up the phone after Nathan started the car. Nathan answered the first beep since he was wearing the headphones. He had put them on as soon as he got in the car.

"You old dog, you," Anderson teased. "You were flirting with her!"

"And you said that to say what?" Nathan injected smiling. "I wondered how long it was gonna take you to speak on it."

"Nate, I've known you a long time, Man. I've never known you to miss someone's age like that. You were off by a mile. You **do** know that, don't you?"

Instead of answering, Nathan threw back his head and roared with laughter. Then he maneuvered the limo around the corner.

"And what was that 'it is not often my eyes grace such an elegant sight...' stuff? Man, oh man, where did that come from?"

"Did you take notes, Son?" Now, Nathan was doing the teasing. "Did you see how it's done? I say, did you learn from the master?" Nathan asked in an animated character's voice. "I say, I may be old, Son, but I ain't dead! Trust me on that one, okay? Besides, I like her. Yes sir, that's my kinda woman, a triple-S."

"Triple-S?" Anderson asked.

"Yeah. Short, smart and sassy. Yes indeed, that's my kinda woman!" Nathan laughed a hearty laugh and Anderson joined him. The two of them enjoyed the exchange for a few more minutes and then Nathan got serious when he spoke again.

"So, Boss? Are we going to school today?" Nathan asked.

"Stop calling me 'Boss'," Anderson said pretending to scold. Then he paused in thought. "No Nate, I don't think so. When we get back to the office, call the school and arrange it for tomorrow and Wednesday," Anderson told him.

"Wednesday too, huh?" Nathan queried, his eyes smiling in the mirror.

"Yeah, Wednesday too. I want to make sure she knows we were there," Anderson told him.

"And you called **me** a dog," Nathan teased.

They both laughed again, enjoying the moment. Then when things grew quiet, Anderson raised the glass partition between them. He settled back in the car's seat and closed his eyes. The image of Gabrielle asleep on the very same seat flashed across his mind. He smiled at that image and then, he saw her mother's pleading eyes again. He really wanted to help her. He **had to** help her. He was still not sure what he would do but he would do something and he would start this week.

CHAPTER V

Nathan Sharpe, the security half of Rayzor-Sharpe Security and Private Investigations, Inc. had grown up with Anderson's father. They had gone through school together since sixth grade. There wasn't a day that went by that you did not find one of them over the other one's house. Both families accepted them as sons and watched and supported them in their endeavors. It was hard to know where one family stopped and the other one began because they were so immersed in each other's lives.

Clayton Ray, Anderson's father, aspired to become a career military man while Nathan wanted to work with the Federal Bureau of Investigation. Both of them had big dreams for the future. Clayton's dreams abruptly came to a halt; Nathan's took a detour.

Nathan was the one Clayton confided in when he found out he was going to be a father. Clayton Ray was adamant about running interference on any plans to have the baby aborted so Nathan suggested the alternative. Once Clayton decided to raise Anderson as a single parent, Nathan offered his help and support. This is how Anderson got his first name. Anderson is Nathan's middle name. They had agreed to name one of their children after each other. It seemed only natural that Anderson considered this man to be his "Uncle Nate."

Uncle Nate took his responsibility as a godfather seriously too. Occasionally baby-sitting to give Clayton or his father a break, he also took Anderson to ball games, the movies or amusement parks. Nathan taught Anderson how to beat his father as chess and trained him in the African Martial Art of Vita Sana.

Nathan went into the Air Force right out of high school. He established a trust fund for his godson right away. He was always bringing Anderson something from places he visited.

Next to his father, Anderson thought the sun rose and set at his uncle's command. Nathan changed his mind about remaining in the service when Clayton was killed. He got a job with a local security agency and learned more about the business. He added to what he had learned in the military and eventually started his own security firm, Sharpe Security Service.

Anderson had closed his eyes to relax. He always liked it when Nathan drove the car because he could take moments like this to unwind. Nate loved to drive so Anderson would acquiesce to Nate whenever his uncle-godfather wanted to get behind the wheel. Nate even freelanced as a chauffeur once in a while. He especially liked prom time, weddings and Mother's Day. When Anderson and Nathan became business partners, Nathan arranged a special Mother's Day Raffle. The winner received the limo and driver for three hours and complimentary champagne. At ten dollars per raffle ticket, Nathan's favorite charity received four hundred and fifty dollars.

Anderson opened his eyes and rubbed his temples. Reflecting on events of the morning, he had to smile. So, Nathan liked Brandeis and she obviously had similar feelings for him; this had possibilities. Anderson looked at the man driving the limousine with admiration and respect. He smiled too because Nathan was wearing a chauffeur's cap. Even though Anderson considered his uncle-godfather a full partner in their company, Nathan liked the facade he'd created.

Anderson had objected about Nathan assuming the role of chauffeur, but Nathan had his own logic on the matter. He told Anderson that because he was a big man, posing as a chauffeur helped him to blend into the surroundings or with the scenery, especially during some of their surveillance jobs. Their merger two years ago had been the best thing to happen to Sharpe Security Agency. Their skills complimented each other.

Anderson turned on his laptop computer and typed several notes to himself. By the time Nathan had pulled up to the hi-rise building on City Avenue that housed their office, Anderson had done half the day's work.

The two men got off the elevator at the fifth floor and walked toward their office. It was not as big as some of the other offices in the building but the two-room facility was big enough to make them look quite impressive. Nathan generally sat at the outer office desk. The walls held three certificates for security, criminology and computer courses. There were shelves holding plaques and trophies for marital arts training and tournaments. There were several file cabinets and all sorts of locks, regular keys, key-blanks and alarms in locked cabinets all over the room. The more elaborate security systems equipment was not in plain view.

Anderson had an adjoining office. His was a bit more fancy with rich redwood paneling on the walls. These walls had shelving, which displayed trophies and framed certificates as well as Anderson's college degree in Criminal Justice/Criminology.

As they approached the outer office door, Nathan's security antenna went up.

He immediately pulled his revolver and stepped in front of Anderson. Anderson stepped back, not because he was incapable of taking care of himself, but because he respected Nathan's ability to do his job. A quick examination of the front door revealed that the lock had been jimmied. In order to break into the office, the person had to also override the security code Nathan had incorporated in the locking system. Carefully, Nathan stepped into the office. Anderson, with his gun drawn also, stepped in behind him. The two men stood back to back for a few minutes examining the area within their line of vision. Satisfied that the person who had broken into the office was now gone, they both holstered their weapons and assessed the damage.

There were papers everywhere! Several things had been moved. File folders had been emptied all over the floor. No equipment had been stolen but the room was a mess. Anderson entered his office and found it in the same condition. His file cabinet drawers had been left open and there were file folders on the desk, in the leather chair and all over the floor. Anderson became anxious and started checking the names on the folders. He returned to the outer office frowning. Nathan had just finished calling building security and the local police to report the break-in. He was hanging up the phone when Anderson walked in. He saw the frown on Anderson's face and one appeared on his own.

"What's missing, Air?" he asked.

"Actually nothing," Anderson told him, "except the file I started since we began searching for my mother."

Nathan looked around the room one more time and started making notes to give the police when they arrived. He also made a note to upgrade their security system. Someone had been sharp enough to bypass the door and he was now going to make certain that it did not happen again.

Anderson took a seat on the leather loveseat that was cater-corner to Nathan's desk.

"Obviously, someone does not want me to find my mother," Anderson replied pensively and then he put his head in his hands.

Nathan nodded. He got up and walked around his desk. He put his hand on his godson's shoulder. He felt it give, even under the slight pressure. Anderson covered his eyes. All the work they had done and someone had wiped it out in a matter of minutes. He knew Anderson was feeling frustrated. One of the reasons his namesake had gone into private investigation was to find the woman who had called him "an inconvenience."

All of a sudden, Nathan remembered something. He went to one of his file cabinets and looking way in the back of the top drawer, pulled out a box of diskettes. To anyone else's eye, this looked like a box of unused disks and this was intentional. Most of the used ones were stored in cases in a locked desk drawer. Nathan reached in the box he was holding.

"I believe you can probably use this right about now," Nathan said looking at Anderson smiling. Anderson looked up. Nathan handed him the only labeled disk from the box. There was only one word written on the label "CASSI."

Anderson recognized the name. It was the code name they had given to his mother's file since her name was Cassandra. Anderson's father had told him that he used to call her Cassi during their high school romance. It was also the only thing Clayton Ray had given Anderson from his mother. When he spelled Cassi backwards, he decided to name his son Isaac.

Anderson was surprised. "What's this?" he asked with his eyes full of hope.

"Well," Nathan began, "since we have a high school and a college student come in on alternating days, I've had them transfer some of our files to disks. I assigned this file to the college student, Kareem. I told him this was high priority and to copy everything you had in the files to this disk and keep it confidential. Since he's pre-law and I had him checked out, I figured we could trust him with the task."

Anderson's face lit up. It was as if someone had shined a light in a dark hole where he had been for the last fifteen minutes. He got up and hugged his uncle-godfather. Then, he went into his office to see if all the information he had gathered was on the disk. When Nathan heard him holler "Yes" a few minutes later, he knew that they were still on track.

While Anderson was scanning the disk's information, Nathan popped the surveillance tape into the VCR. He did not mention it to Anderson because he wanted to see whose face came up on the screen first. Their burglar was sharp enough to bypass a security lock, but he never looked up to notice the security camera. Then again, due to Nathan's ingenuity, it was not in plain sight. Nathan looked hard but he did not recognize

37

the face he saw. The light-skinned, Hispanic looking male who came up on the TV screen was young, probably in his mid-twenties. He had wavy brown hair and long sideburns. Comparing his height to that of the file cabinets, Nathan judged the young man to be about five-seven. He was medium build, probably about one-sixty-five or one hundred-seventy pounds.

"I think you'd better see this," Nathan called over his shoulder.

"Why, what's up?" Anderson asked coming out of his office. He walked closer to Nathan and frowned. The guy on the screen had momentarily turned to the file cabinets and was pulling on drawers; some were easier to open than others. When he got to the locked door to Anderson's office, he swore out loud. Looking around for something to aid in his break-in his face was turned toward the camera although he never spotted it. Anderson looked harder.

"Well I'll be..." Anderson said in amazement, raising one eyebrow.

"I take it you recognize him?" Nathan asked.

"Yeah," Anderson replied, "although I have no idea why he would want my mother's file."

"So, who the heck is he?" Nathan asked anxiously.

"He's the guy I told you about. The one at the train station with the BMW. His name is..." He paused as if he could not believe he had to say it, "Jimmy."

"And the plot thickens," Nathan said thinking out loud. "Want me to check him out?" He turned to Anderson who now had an angry frown.

"Yeah. Since he's already seen me, I think you could be more effective and I need to know what this turkey is up to," Anderson said still looking at the tape. His anger was seething.

They replayed the tape again and made a duplicate. They put the original in an envelope to give the police when they arrived. In the meantime, Nathan took some fingerprints using ultraviolet light around the file cabinet area. The surface of the cabinets had been treated with a special solution the day they were moved into the office. He had just finished and had put his equipment away by the time the local police arrived. Nathan and Anderson answered all the questions during the initial police report but they did not admit knowing the identity of the burglar. They decided they might get more help from the police if they withheld that piece of information until later. After the police left, Nathan started making the phone calls that would begin his own investigation.

CHAPTER VI

Gabrielle was not able to return to work on Tuesday as planned. She had to take another sick day because cleaning the apartment all day Monday had left her exhausted and she was still sore. Even though she had prepared a romantic dinner for two, Jimmy did not come home on Monday night. When he finally came in Tuesday morning, they had another heated argument and Jimmy used that as an excuse to leave again. Once Jimmy stormed back out of the apartment, Gabrielle cried herself to sleep. Most of Tuesday went by in a blur as a day of mechanical tasks.

Gabrielle did not even call her mother to ask her how the Career Week presentation went. She knew that if her mother talked about her baking business and took the children cookies, the day went well. Gabrielle stayed in the apartment all day and let the answering machine take messages.

At four o'clock in the afternoon, she turned on the television in the living room. She was channel surfing with the remote control when a talk show caught her interest. The topic of the program was Abusive, Controlling Men and How to Spot Them.

The main person that got Gabrielle's attention was a very tired looking, middle-age woman named Ruby. She spoke of an abusive relationship with a man named Adam. She was telling the audience that a good bit of the abuse she suffered was mental and emotional.

"When I first met Adam, he was Mr. Wonderful. I guess I would say that he pampered and spoiled me. He used to compliment me on everything. He said he admired how smart I was, how talented I was. I had my own business and it was doing well when we met. I was a little self-conscious about my weight but he said he liked his women with a little meat on their bones. He said he loved me and that he couldn't live without me. I guess, I should have been suspicious because he poured it on

*heavy so early in our relationship but after having to break off
an engagement a few years earlier, I thought I had finally found
a good man. When I think of how wonderful he was when we
first met and how mean he became, I can't believe it was the
same person."*

Ruby was crying when the program went to a commercial
break and so was Gabrielle. She was a little nervous about
Jimmy coming home but figured that he would not be in until
after dark. She went in the kitchen, fixed herself a cup of tea and
grabbed some tissues. When she returned to the living room,
Ruby was speaking again.

*"Adam never really hit me. He just pulled and yanked me
around; grabbing my arm and my hair. Once, he even dragged
me by my ankle after I fell down. I was trying to get away from
him during an argument. I fell. He called me clumsy and
grabbed my ankle and just started walking."*

*"During sex, he was always mean. He never kissed me or
held me. He said he didn't have time for that stuff and if that's
what I wanted, I should get a teddy bear!"*

The audience moaned and Gabrielle winced remembering
some of Jimmy's cruel words during their six months together.

*"No, he was never gentle with me when we were intimate. He
laughed if I tried to tell him what I wanted. I don't think he cared
what I wanted. He just did what he wanted to do and went to
sleep."*

Ruby had shredded the tissues she was holding. Her voice
was shaky but she struggled to continue.

*"My business went down the tubes. I had a designer dress
shop. My specialty was one-of-a-kind gowns. My family had
helped me open it so, I know they were disappointed when I had
to file for bankruptcy. I think my brother was more disappointed
than anybody, except maybe me. Even though I worked for
myself, I had regular hours that my shop was open. Adam would
cause me to open late, miss appointments...sometimes I'd be too
tired to go in. He even complained that my business was*

*interfering with our love life. My business was keeping a roof over our heads but **he** complained about our love life."*

"Our love life!" Ruby shrieked, *"what love life? I'd hardly call what we had a relationship."* She swallowed hard. So did Gabrielle. Ruby looked directly at the camera. Gabrielle jumped as if Ruby were looking at her. Sad eyes, that's what Gabrielle saw looking out at her from the screen. She shivered as she remembered looking in the mirror Monday morning, bruised and sore. She had caught her reflection in the mirror as she passed on her way to the bathroom and saw sad eyes looking back at her.

Ruby was crying again as she continued her story.

"One night, Adam came in very drunk and after he finished with me, he passed out. I dressed in sweats and with the overnight bag I'd packed and hidden earlier that day, I snuck out the door. I went down to the corner and called my brother from a pay phone. He came and got me and took me to my mom's."

"But that wasn't the end of it, was it Ruby?" the talk show host asked probingly.

*"No, because Adam came after me. The first time, he followed me home from work and dragged me back to our apartment. He kept saying that he owned me...**owned me**! He really believed that and it was frightening."*

"Ruby, you said 'the first time you left...'?" the host gently urged her to continue.

"Oh, I left three times," Ruby replied weakly.

"Well, we know the second time didn't work either. Tell us what happened."

"I got that stupid piece of paper. What's it called? A restraining order? Just so you women know, they don't work because men like Adam ignore them," Ruby said angrily. She dabbed her eyes with a new tissue.

"Anyway, I got the restraining order and the police went with me to the apartment the day I moved out the rest of my things. He received his order to report to court the day after I left for the second time. After the hearing, where he denied

everything by the way; I went to work. I had gotten a job by then. Adam was waiting for me that afternoon. I didn't see him at first. A friend drove me to the boarding home where I had rented a room. Adam followed us in his car. By the time my co-worker had driven away, Adam was running toward the porch. I screamed as I fought to keep from going with him. That was the first time he hit me. If it wasn't for the landlady, I don't know what might have happened."

Gabrielle did not want to hear any more. Ruby's story had too many similarities to her own. It could have been her life unfolding on that program. Yet, Gabrielle found herself riveted to the television screen.

"Thank God, the police came," Ruby continued, *"when they took Adam away he kept yelling at me. 'No one can have you. No one. No one. You're mine, do you hear me? Mine! I still remember how he said it...remember how he looked at me. It still makes my shiver."*

Ruby did shiver and sob. She dabbed her eyes and the program had another commercial. Gabrielle started to call her mother but so much of Ruby's story had already been told, she decided against it. Gabrielle busied herself making the room neat even though nothing was really out of place. She wanted a distraction from the program even though she could not bring herself to turn the television off. When she heard Ruby's voice again, she went back to the loveseat.

"Adam spent forty-eight hours in jail; then he was out on bail with a warning. He changed his tactics after that. He started calling me at the job several times a day, begging me to talk to him...telling me he loved me. He sent gifts to the job...flowers, candy, cards, jewelry and lingerie. He even sent a ring with a message saying he wanted to marry me. He couldn't bring the ring up himself because I gave security instructions not to let him in no matter what he said. He hated that. He made sure I knew that every time he called. He told me I was being unfair.

It was so crazy. One minute, he'd be begging, pleading with me to come back to him...telling me he needed me in his life. When I refused, he'd turn into this raging madman, calling me names...telling me I was fat and ugly and that no one would want me. He even said I was lucky he wanted to be bothered with my sorry..." Ruby started crying again.

Gabrielle was stunned. She looked at the television screen and could not contain her emotions. When the tears flowed, she let them. When Ruby sobbed, so did Gabrielle. Gabrielle shook her head once or twice in disbelief during some of Ruby's story but she continued to sit and listen. Ruby's eyes were red and swollen when the camera did a close-up. Gabrielle stared at the woman who seemed to be looking at her.

"It was all about control and with some help from a counselor and my pastor, I took control of my life again. It was not easy. I'd be lying if I sat here and said it was. Adam seemed to be everywhere for a while. He wouldn't understand that I did not want him in my life anymore."

"Where is he now, Ruby?" the program host asked.

"In jail!" Ruby answered firmly. *"He'd been stalking me for a while and I'd get these hang up calls. I was home alone one night and he broke in. that's when he beat me so bad I had to go to the hospital. But I thank God for my Brother..."* *"My brother Nathan, the one who helped me; he works in security and he made sure Adam wouldn't bother me ever again."* The audience applauded and there were shouts of "Way to go, Nathan!"

"So Ruby, it sounds like you and your brother are close?" The host asked.

"We're a lot closer now," Ruby stated with her first smile. *"I think he was disgusted with me for a while. I mean, I'd call him, begging for his help only to go back to Adam over and over again. I can even remember one time; I called him and Nathan flat out said 'NO!' I couldn't blame him. I mean, it must have*

been frustrating when people who love you reach out to help and..." Ruby could not finish the thought.

"I'm sure it has not been easy, putting your life back together," the host added, sympathetically.

"No, it hasn't," Ruby answered, *"but it's MY life and that's the part I had forgotten for a while. Also, I had to remember that there are people who really care about me and were willing to be there for me. I don't need a man so much that it should destroy me."* Ruby gave another half smile and the audience applauded again.

"Is there anything you want to say to the audience or the people watching?"

Ruby looked up and the camera moved in closer. She took a deep breath and swallowed.

*"When people look at me, they see a woman about forty-three years old, except that I'm **not** forty-three. I'm only thirty-five! I've aged about eight years in eleven months. My nerves got so bad my hair fell out. I was always looking over my shoulder, paralyzed with fear. I was robbed of part of my life; things I care about, people I love, friends and the worst part is that I **let** him take it all from me."*

Ruby paused for a minute. *"If any of this sounds familiar. If any of my life sounds like yours, you've got some serious thinking to do. There are good times and bad times in a relationship, but love is **not** violent. If you need help to leave, get help. If you can leave, get out while the getting is good. **Get out NOW!**"*

Ruby dropped her eyes. The host went to put her arms around Ruby and the audience gave her a standing ovation. The host turned to the audience to do her sign off.

"There you have it folks, sound advice from one who has been there. If you need help, check the numbers at the bottom of your screen and remember...

Gabrielle turned off the television and sat staring at the blank screen.

Brandeis was sitting in her kitchen sipping a hot cup of herbal tea. The NEWS was on the television but she was not watching and just barely listening. She wiped her eyes and added another tissue to the pile in the trash can in the corner. Brandeis had just finished watching her favorite talk show, "TAKE CHARGE" with Stacey Amison. She tried never to miss the program because Stacey always has someone on the show with an interesting story. However, when she heard the topic for this program: Abusive and Controlling Men, Brandeis almost changed the channel. She was in no mood to hear anything that sounded like Gabrielle's situation or her past life.

Brandeis reached for the remote as the talk show host introduced her guest using her first name only. Brandeis stopped her hand in mid-motion. What she saw was a woman who bore a striking resemblance to Nathan Sharpe! This woman had the same red-brown coloring, high-rounded cheekbones and those deep dimples. They were the main things that caught Brandeis's eye when the woman gave a weak, half smile. *She's pretty*, Brandeis thought, *but she does look like she's been through hell.*

When the woman named Ruby began to speak, Brandeis was impressed by her courage. One had to be strong to tell this story. One had to be strong to live through it!

Brandeis sat back to listen to what became a heart-wrenching story. As she continued to listen, she was struck with wonder. Ruby kept mentioning a man named Nathan. Was the man Ruby called her brother Nathan, the same man who had been standing in her living room just yesterday? They had not talked in depth about family but this woman looked like she could indeed be his sister. If it was true, it would explain why these two men would willingly help her. She had no doubt that Anderson would tell his partner about her daughter, Gabrielle.

When the program ended, Brandeis sat quietly with tears streaming down her face. Her heart went out to the woman on the program but at the same time, she felt a personal peace inside. This woman had survived her experience; somehow she knew Gabrielle would too.

CHAPTER VII

When Gabrielle returned to work on Wednesday, the third graders were buzzing about "a big white car." Gabrielle listened as the boys and girls went on and on about the two men who came to their classroom yesterday.

"They took our fingerprints and gave them to us to take home," said Arnold who wanted to be a police officer when he grew up.

"They showed us a videotape about shoplifters," Betty told her.

"Yeah, and they told us that it's wrong to steal because the owners of the stores pay for the stuff so when they sell it to us they can get their money back and make some money," said Angie as she smiled under her freckles.

"That's right, Angie. It is wrong to steal because it would be taking something away from someone else," Gabrielle assured her.

Gabrielle was practically surrounded by the class and they all wanted to tell her about the secur'ty man and the private 'vestigater who came to the class yesterday.

"We're all gonna get...uh...gonna get..." Monique was making faces trying hard to remember something.

"I-D cards," Brad said from the corner of the room. He always sat in a corner trying not to be noticed.

Gabrielle looked up and toward the corner. Bradley Mitchell was the shyest student in the class but he was also one of the smartest. Gabrielle usually had to coax him to say anything during class work, but she had succeeded where others had not.

"Yeah," answered Monique in agreement, "I Deek cards."

"That's I- D cards, Monique," Gabrielle corrected.

"That's what I said," Monique said confidently.

Everybody laughed including Gabrielle, then she walked over to Brad. She touched the top of his head. She smiled at him and pulled up a chair so he would not have to look up so far to talk to her. He smiled back very slowly.

"That was very good, Bradley." Gabrielle was the only one allowed to call him Bradley. "You have such a good memory," she told him. Brad blushed and turned his face to the wall.

"Aw Bradley," cooed Gabrielle, "I came over here so you could tell me more about yesterday." She feigned a pout and the students looked from Gabrielle to Brad and back again.

"The big guy, Mr. Nathan...uh...I mean Mr. Sharpe, told us about dangerous strangers," Brad told her. "He said there are people who tell stories to get kids to go with them. He said sometimes they say that they lost a pet or sometimes they will tell you that they're lost and can't find an address."

"Yeah," said Monique who had a secret crush on Brad. "Mr. Nathan said that sometimes the bad people will tell you that you have to go with them because your mother wants you. Sometimes they even tell you that somebody in your family is sick and they want you to go with them to a neighbor's house."

"But Mr. Sharpe said that most of the time, it's not true and we should never go with them. We should run away as fast as we can." Brad gave a nod and turned his face away.

Monique nodded and folded her arms across her chest and Brad turned back to look at her. She smiled at him and he turned his face again. *My goodness,* Gabrielle thought, *this man made quite an impression yesterday.*

"Well, I don't care what nobody says," piped up Tiffany with her hands on her hips, "them Brothahs was fine, especially the bald one!"

"Those Brothers were fine," Gabrielle corrected before she realized what she was saying. The class giggled and Gabrielle put her hand up to her mouth. *Bald One? Who is she talking about?*

"Yes, they were," stated Tiffany emphatically.

"Oo-o-o, Tiffany," said Betty with a shocked expression that only an eight-year-old could have.

"You said it too, Betty," Brad reminded her, causing Betty to make a face of disappointment because she had been found out.

"What was really cool," exclaimed Jamal with his eyes widened in amazement, "was when Mr. Ray took us out to look at the big car. That's one mean machine." The other students agreed while different degrees of wonder shown on their faces.

"Wait a minute," Gabrielle said frowning suddenly. "Did you say 'Mr. Ray'?"

"Uh-huh," Jamal said nodding. The rest of the students nodded too.

Just then Ms. Parker entered the classroom and the students went back to their seats. Some of them were unhappy because they had not gotten a chance to tell Gabrielle about yesterday. Ms. Parker lowered her wire-framed glasses to the tip of her pug nose and looked out at her class. They always laughed when she did that.

She was a thirty-year-old woman with a sandy complexion and medium brown hair that she always wore in a ponytail. She had been teaching for six years. Her class loved her because her teaching went beyond classroom curriculum.

"My goodness, why all the long faces?" she asked looking at fifteen of the saddest expressions she had ever seen.

"The children were telling me about the exciting day they had yesterday," Gabrielle informed her in a special animated voice. It was part of a routine the two of them went through when it was "Let's Talk About It Time." This could happen at any time so Gabrielle and Mrs. Parker stayed tuned into each other in order to know when it should happen. Gabrielle knew by the looks on all their faces that the class wanted to talk now.

"Well then," Ms. Parker began in her animated old lady voice as she rubbed her hands together, "let's talk about it!"

Immediately, hands shot up all over the classroom. Once again, one by one, the boys and girls described everything they remembered from the day before. After about an hour, the class went into their regular class work. Gabrielle assisted Ms. Parker with the lessons by giving out or collecting papers or books. She took some students to another room to read to them, and then she had some of them read to her. She escorted them to music class and later they went outside for recess.

It was during recess that Gabrielle caught sight of Brad when he wandered away from the class and went to stand by the schoolyard gate. While Ms. Parker watched the rest of the class playing, Gabrielle walked over to Brad.

"Bradley, you know you have to stay with the class. What are you looking at?" she asked when she realized that he was not listening. Then she saw it too. The white limousine.

"They're back," Brad said voicing her thought out loud.

"Do you think they'll come back to our class?" His eyes held an anxious expression when he looked up at Gabrielle.

"I don't know, Sweetie," she replied as she stooped down and put her arm around his shoulder, "but we need to go back to the other part of the schoolyard."

He put his hand in hers and they joined the class. Brad told Monique who told everyone else that he had seen the limo and the class surrounded him. Ms. Parker saw the terrified look that came over Brad's face and stepped into the circle of students. She had them line up to return to class. Instantly, Brad looked relieved. Everyone got in line to go back inside but still tried craning their tiny necks to see where the limousine was parked. Gabrielle too, was straining to get one more look at the "big car."

For the rest of the morning, she had a hard time concentrating on schoolwork. Her thoughts kept wandering to the man with the dynamic, dark-brown eyes and silky-smooth, deep voice. *And who is Mr. Nathan?* she pondered curiously.

It was almost noon. Anderson and Nathan were relaxing in the teachers' lounge. They had finished their last presentation of the day. The two of them had visited two fourth and a fifth grade class. The students had been attentive, courteous and inquisitive. Their interest had been genuine. The boys and girls seemed proud to meet two African-American men who were entrepreneurs in their particular line of work. Their presentation and talk with the older students was more sophisticated than it had been with the third graders. This time the focus was more on Anderson's work in private investigation. The students wanted to know what kind of cases he investigated. They asked about the hardest case and the most interesting. He told them that he especially liked the cases where he found missing persons and the reunions with the family members were happy ones.

Nathan had done most of the talking on Tuesday in Gabrielle's class. The younger students had been fascinated by the gadgets like the master key that could open many locks. They also liked being fingerprinted and posing for identification cards. Nathan gave them many tips on being safe, coming to school or going home.

Anderson sat sipping a cup of hot tea. He had taken off his burgundy blazer and loosened his black and burgundy striped tie. He unfastened the top button of his white shirt that was tucked neatly in his gray slacks. Nathan wore a similar outfit but his pants were black and his shirt was a pale yellow. The third graders had noticed Anderson's belt buckle because of the silver lightening bolt in the center. Nathan had one too. His was gold. They had explained to the class that the buckles were custom made when they celebrated the first anniversary of Rayzor-Sharpe Security and Private Investigations, Inc. Anderson grinned as he remembered how excited the children got when Nathan asked them to guess how their company got its name.

Each child who guessed accurately received a pencil with the company logo on it. Anderson had to smile because he did not even know that Nathan had purchased them. Some of the children figured out that "Ray" was Anderson's last name and "Sharpe" was Nathan's last name. Anderson had written the name of the company on the blackboard and crossed out the portions the children guessed correctly. The only thing left was z-o-r. Nathan asked again if anyone could guess how it came to be part of the name of their company. Nathan said he knew this was the hardest part so he promised a special prize to the student who guessed correctly.

From the back of the class had come a quiet little voice and when Nathan heard it, he had to ask all the other students to settle down. Nathan walked all the way to the back of the class and got down on one knee beside Brad's desk. For a few moments neither of them spoke and once Nathan made eye contact with Brad, he smiled. Brad's eyes widened. Nathan's dimples were so deep Brad had to reach out and touch one.

Brad smiled back and said "your beard tickles" then he laughed.

"No kidding," said Nathan and he laughed. The class laughed too.

Once everyone was quiet, Nathan asked Brad to repeat what he said earlier. Nathan was wearing a Lapel Mic and asked Brad to speak into it. Brad was hesitant at first but with some encouragement he finally agreed.

"Well," Brad began, leaning near Nathan's shoulder, "you did say that when you were young, you watched Zorro on TV a lot. You said that he was your hero. You said that your father used to say that you were 'sharp as a razor.' Then, you said when you went to high school; you were on the fencing team so I just thought, maybe..." He didn't finish so Nathan helped him.

"It seem that you are very good at processing information and that's what we do in our jobs, process the facts we get. So, guess what, my man, you are absolutely right!" Nathan said enthusiastically, "and that is why our lightning bolt is shaped like the letter 'Z'." The class applauded. Then, Nathan reached inside his jacket and pulled a black and gold pen from his pocket and handed it to Brad. Brad beamed with pride as the class "oo-oowed" and "ah-ahhed" in envious surprise especially when they noticed the company logo on it. Even Anderson was taken aback and raised an eyebrow when he saw his godfather give up his favorite pen.

Nathan shook Brad's hand before walking back to the front of the class. *Yes, this had been an interesting beginning to the week,* Anderson thought reflecting on the first few days, and *this is only Wednesday.*

Anderson looked over at his mentor who was seated on the sofa in the corner of the teachers' lounge. Nathan had dozed off. Anderson was tired, so he knew Nathan was too. It was a glorious tired because they had done what they enjoyed doing, interacting with young people.

Anderson was about to wake his partner when Gabrielle rushed into the room. She stopped dead in her tracks when she saw him. Her hazel eyes widened and she swallowed hard trying to catch her breath. Anderson smiled at her as he rose from his seat.

"Well hello," he said as his smile eased into a grin. He reached out his hand in her direction.

"Hi," she managed in a voice she hoped was not too loud. She was afraid the beat of her heart was drowning her out.

"I'm glad I caught you before you left," she told him once she had taken a deep breath. She extended her hand to take his.

"So am I. We missed you yesterday." They only touched fingertips before she pulled back. She did not want to let on that she liked what he had just said. *We missed you yesterday. We?* she thought. She was about to speak when Nathan shifted position while sleeping.

Gabrielle turned her head in the direction of the noise. She remembered what Tiffany had said. *The Bald One!* she realized. Oh yes, Tiffany had been quite correct in her assessment.

"Mr. Nathan?" Gabrielle declared with an open hand in the sleeping man's direction, since she had taught the students that it was not polite to point.

"Mr. Nathan **Sharpe**," Anderson added using one hand in the same gesture.

"What are you two doing?" Nathan asked sitting up. He was a light sleeper and opened his eyes when he heard his full name. Once he realized that there was a woman in the room, he stood up and extended his hand as Anderson made the introductions.

"Gabrielle Grayson, this is my partner, Nathan Sharpe."

"My pleasure. You are truly as lovely as Air said you were," he told her. He cut his eyes to Anderson with a *now we're even* look while Anderson looked at him as if he wanted to hit him.

Gabrielle's eyes widened in surprise from the revelation that at some point, she had been the topic of conversation. She blushed as she shook Nathan's hand and then dropped her eyes. Nathan leaned down to catch her eye and when she looked up again, he smiled revealing his deep dimples.

"No on second thought," he said with a slight frown, "I don't think Air was completely accurate." Gabrielle looked puzzled. "You are much prettier in person," he told her and once again his broad smile appeared. He cut his eyes at Anderson once more. Anderson had folded his arms across his chest and had one hand under his chin. He covered his mouth at Nathan's remark and frowned as his mentor grinned back at him.

Gabrielle cleared her throat when she did not know how to respond and changed the subject. "It seems the two of you made quite an impression in my class yesterday." She took a seat at the table in the center of the room. Nathan and Anderson joined her.

"Brad was completely taken with you," she continued. "He's always been a bit of an introvert and his shyness has been what blocks his participation in class sometimes. He's very bright though, so we try to encourage him without pushing. Naomi, I mean Ms. Parker, tells me that yesterday Brad was a bundle of knowledge when you asked questions."

She turned to look at Nathan who nodded while rubbing his chin. He was listening intently and pleased he had been helpful.

"Brad is a smart little guy," he affirmed.

"What made you take to him the way you did or was it the other way around? Did you sense something in particular?"

"No, not really. He just reminded me of someone else who was like that at Brad's age," Nathan told her and turned to look at Anderson.

"What?" Anderson sat up straight in his seat since he was suddenly being scrutinized by both of them. Gabrielle nodded with understanding and Anderson shrugged his shoulders.

"What?" he said again looking around.

"Grayson? Grayson," Nathan said slowly as if trying to remember something. "Hey Air, do I...?"

"Yeah," Anderson cut in, "this is Brandeis's daughter."

Nathan looked at her again and noted the resemblance. "Well, how about that. I've met the daughter of the gem. Your mother is quite a lady." Gabrielle looked confused.

"He met your mother on Monday," Anderson informed her.

Gabrielle did not say anything but in her mind she could not help wondering what transpired on Monday. She had a feeling it had been a very interesting meeting.

Just then the school buzzer sounded and Gabrielle immediately looked at her watch.

"OOPS, gotta go. I've got lunchroom duty."

"Want some help?" Nathan asked.

Gabrielle's eyes widened and she looked from one man to the other. "Are you kidding?" She asked anxiously. "Please, don't tease. We're always short-handed at lunchtime."

"That's what I figured," Nathan answered, "Besides, I know a little about how much of a handful kids can be." He turned and looked at Anderson.

"What?" Anderson shrugged. When no one said anything, Anderson walked toward the door. "Okay, but we're only doing this for you," he told Gabrielle. Nathan made a "tsk, tsk" noise and shook his head and then he smiled at them.

When the three of them entered the room full of second and third graders, half of the students were already seated. The rest of the students were in line waiting to get their lunch.

As soon as Gabrielle's class saw the two men who came into the room, they cheered. Then, with urging from Tiffany, the boys and girls started a rhythmic chant of "ho-oh, hey-ay, ho-oh, hey-ay." Nathan broke into a dance similar to the "Tootsie Roll" and the student laughed. After a few minutes, he put two fingers in his mouth and whistled. The entire room got quiet. In a fatherly tone, he told the students to make their teachers proud and settle down. There wasn't another sound throughout the cafeteria. Then, he told them that they could talk to their friends as long as they did it in low tones. He walked around and started shaking hands with students. He smiled. They smiled and lunchtime was very pleasant. Gabrielle, Ms. Parker and Anderson exchanged glances. They were all impressed. Nathan Sharpe and kids, the combination was sheer magic. Nathan even took a minute to say a special hello to Brad who became all smiles during lunch and for the rest of the day.

Teachers and volunteers took different posts in the room. They also walked around a few tables to make sure everyone cleaned up before leaving their seats to go to the bathroom or out in the school yard to play.

A boy from a second grade class got up from his seat and darted toward the door. He found himself stopped in mid-stride. He raised his head to see what blocked his way and had to lift his eyes almost to the ceiling. He was face to face with Anderson's frown. Anderson stood in a wide stance blocking the door to the schoolyard, arms folded and looking down at the little guy. Other students giggled and smirked at the sight before they turned their faces away but not without taking an occasional peek and snickering again. Anderson looked toward some of them and put his finger to his lips. The room silenced as he crouched down in front of the boy.

"Say, my man," Anderson said in a friendly tone. He put his hand on the boy's shoulder and the student noticed how big this man's hand was. "Do you leave a mess at home?"

"No sir," the boy replied emphatically then swallowed.

It only took a look so when Anderson raised an eyebrow, the boy walked back to his seat and cleaned up everything. He stacked his tray properly and even helped two friends. He cleaned up any napkins, paper wrappers and cartons; putting them in recycle bins and sat back in his seat. Anderson walked over to him and put his hand on the boy's shoulder. When the little guy turned around and looked up Anderson was smiling. The big man stooped down and held up his hand. The boy blew out a breath of relief and gave him a high-five. The boy ran past Anderson and out the door to the schoolyard. Gabrielle covered her mouth, but when Anderson looked in her direction, he could tell she was laughing. When he shrugged his shoulders and gave her a "raspberry," she laughed harder.

The scene between Anderson and the second grader started a chain reaction. All the students cleaned up their areas, stacked their trays properly and threw away any trash they found. Then they went outside to play. All of the teachers looked at Nathan and Anderson with gratitude. Gabrielle walked over to Anderson.

"My goodness, we should have you two here all the time."

"Well ma'am," Anderson replied, faking a Southern drawl, "I reckon we do what we kin."

He stepped aside and she joined her class outside. Ms. Parker went up to the classroom to prepare the homework assignment for the class. Anderson and Nathan watched the students line up in the schoolyard.

"Does that bring back memories, Air?" Nathan asked in a serious tone.

Anderson did an exaggerated shiver. "At least I don't have to reach back **too far** to conjure up those memories," he teased.

"Ow, you watch your mouth, Son. I'm still your elder." Nathan made an unpleasant face and shook his head. "Elder…uh." They both laughed and went into the hall.

Gabrielle's class walked by the two men quietly and in a single file. Brad was at the end of the line. He was walking with his head down. Nathan walked over to him. He got in line behind Brad and at first he did not realize Nathan was there. As soon as Brad sensed that someone was behind him, he turned around. When Brad turned, his eyes widened. He almost spoke but Nathan put his finger to his lips cautioning Brad not to make a sound. Nathan took a business card from his breast pocket. He circled a telephone number on it and wrote the words, 'call me anytime you want to talk' on the back. Then, he gave it to Brad. The boy's eyes brightened in surprise again. When he read the message Nathan had written, he gave a toothy grin. Nathan signaled him with his finger to his lips again. Brad nodded covering his mouth and placing the card in his pants pocket. He put his finger to his lips too. Then he disappeared into his classroom.

Anderson, who had observed the whole scene from a distance, stepped forward. The two men headed back to the teachers' lounge in silence.

"That boy has really taken a liking to you, Nate," Anderson said once he had taken a seat on the sofa.

"Yeah," Nathan began in a somber tone. "I like him too. Did you know he lives in a home for boys?" Nathan took a seat on the arm of the same sofa at the opposite end.

"A juvie home?" Anderson said in disbelief.

"No…not a home for bad boys, a home for…abandoned boys," Nathan said with a crack in his voice.

"Get the…"Anderson's head snapped up. He'd almost swore but he remembered something his grandfather had said about what defines and defiles a man and caught himself. His self-respect helped him hold his tongue. Remembering his own childhood and the vague sense of his unfamiliar mother caused his features to darken.

"How did you find out?"

"Ms. Parker told me when the class went outside," Nathan told him. His jaw line hardened.

Anderson knew that his mentor was struggling to hold his emotions together. He suspected that Nathan's feelings were just as mixed as his own. Nathan stared straight ahead. He gave a long exhale before he spoke again.

"Air, I get so mad when I think about people who dispose of their babies like so much unwanted…" Nathan stopped.

In the midst of his anger he had forgotten how tender this subject was with his godson. Nathan slammed his eyes shut. In the old days, he would be cussing himself after making such a blunder, but he had made some promises at the Million Man March that he intended to keep. He rose slowly from his end of the sofa and walked over to Anderson. His godson was sitting forward on the sofa with his elbows bent, and resting on his knees. He had his head in his hands and his eyes were closed. Nathan touched Anderson's shoulder but Anderson did not move.

"Uh, Air…say man, sometimes the old man just doesn't think, you know. I mean…"

"Forget it, Nate. It's okay," Anderson said looking up at him, "I can't go through changes over somebody I've never met. Besides, you and my dad went through more changes than I did." He reached up and shook his uncle-godfather's other hand. "If it wasn't for you, talking to my dad when he needed a friend, I might not even be here." Anderson rose to his feet. They stood eye to eye for a moment. It didn't matter that Anderson was two inches taller. It didn't matter that Nathan was not a blood relative. They stood there, uncle and nephew, godfather and godson, mentor and mentee, partner and senior partner, friend and friend. The handshake held a little longer. Nathan reached out and gave Anderson a fatherly pat on the back and Anderson clipped Nathan's shoulder with a punch. They both laughed to break the tension in the room and headed toward the door.

CHAPTER VIII

Gabrielle was stunned, confused and amazed. The door to the teachers' lounge had not been completely closed, so when she grabbed the doorknob no one heard her. The pain in Nathan's voice as he spoke about children halted her steps. She really had not meant to eavesdrop, but her feet froze where she was. The more they spoke, the more she couldn't move. By the time she could, she could tell by their voices that Nathan and Anderson were headed toward the door. She backed up several steps to give the impression that she had just arrived. She greeted them with her brightest smile.

"Hi you two. It looks like you're leaving now. Are you really going now?"

"'Fraid so," Nathan answered. "This is still a workday for us."

"What about you?" Anderson asked stepping closer to her and smiling.

"Me? I'm done for the day." She had stammered a little and now she was feeling quite self-conscious.

Nathan smiled at the couple and began walking ahead of them. Anderson fell into step with Gabrielle and they all walked toward the front door of the school.

"Do you have a ride home?" he asked when they were outside and walking down the steps.

"Nope. I catch the bus every morning."

"Then, may we give you a ride somewhere?" he asked with hope in his voice and a smile on his face. He touched her hand and his own suddenly got warm.

She started to pull her hand away when she gazed up into those deep brown eyes again. They were sincere, rich, and heavenly. She looked around and after making sure no students were watching, she took hold of his hand and they walked toward the limousine. Nathan was already in the driver's seat, with headphones on and the motor running. Anderson and

Gabrielle got in the car and after closing their rear passenger door, Anderson turned to her and said, "Where to?"

They both burst out laughing after experiencing deja vu. They were still looking at each other when Nathan's voice broke through on the intercom.

"If you please, sir," he said in his best-manufactured British accent, "might I know thy destination? Or wouldst thou stay here and cause gossip? Little eyes and all that, you know." He wriggled his eyebrows up and down and smiled. Suddenly, those captivating deep dimples appeared again and Gabrielle burst out laughing as she looked at his reflection in the rear view mirror.

"How does he do that?" she asked as she turned back to Anderson and tried to stop laughing.

"Both his parents had dimples," Anderson revealed with a shrug, "he just got a double dose, that's all."

"My mother would positively adore you," Gabrielle told Nathan looking toward the front of the luxury car again.

"She already does," Anderson volunteered too quickly. He caught Nathan's disapproval in the mirror.

"Say Air...be cool," Nathan called out as Anderson pressed the button to raise the glass partition to soundproof the rear of the car. Nathan frowned. Anderson smiled at him. Gabrielle looked at Anderson questioningly and he took her hand.

"I'll tell you all about it in a minute," he promised. He picked up the phone and Nathan answered on the first beep.

"Drop me at the office, Nate. Then take Gabrielle wherever she wants to go."

Gabrielle did not hear Nathan's response but she heard Anderson laugh when he said, "Okay, okay only the highlights, all right?" When he hung up, he was still laughing.

"Now," he said turning to Gabrielle, "where were we?"

Gabrielle laughed again. It was a hearty and genuine laugh and he was glad he was the cause of it. "You were about to tell me about the meeting between Nathan **and my mother**."

"Oh yeah, so I was. Well…"

"Anderson?" Gabrielle interrupted. The way she said his name broke his train of thought. Everything stopped but the car. "Anderson," Gabrielle said touching his arm, "would you tell me something first? Why does Nathan call you...'Air'?"

His nickname floated from her mouth as if it were part of a gentle breeze. He replayed the question in his mind a few times before he answered. He looked at her and loved her genuine curiosity. He looked at her and wished Jimmy was a foggy memory. He cleared his throat.

"My initials," he said finally.

"What?"

"My initials."

"What do you mean?" She frowned intently not understanding him.

"My name is Anderson Isaac Ray. A-I-R...Air." He gave her a half smile and glanced out of the window. For some reason, his voice suddenly sounded far away. "Nathan gave me the nickname when I was a baby, when he became my godfather. It was reinforced when he took me on a visit to his grandmother's. I went through an official Blackfoot tribal naming ceremony when I was twelve. I'm known as "Whispering Air."

Gabrielle marveled at the tenderness and reverence in his tone. Anderson got very quiet and Gabrielle thought it best to let him have a few moments to himself.

There was a long pause before he spoke again. Then, he told Gabrielle about the visit to her mother's house. He omitted what Brandeis said about Jimmy. He told her about the mini tour of the house and some of what happened when her mother met Nathan. True to his word, he did not tell the whole story but Gabrielle found the parts he told her, fascinating.

"So-o-o," she began when he was done, "Nathan likes my mother." She had a matchmaker's gleam in her eye.

Anderson raised an eyebrow. "Hey! Whoa!...No need for that," he assured her, "I think they'll do fine on their own."

"But a little help couldn't..." she coaxed.

"Oh no you don't," he told her firmly but at least he was smiling when he said it. "You didn't see what I saw. They don't need any help."

"Are you sure?" she persisted, "I could..."

"Stay out of it, Gabrielle." He only said her name but the tone of his voice and the knit to his eyebrows said more.

"I know that tone and that look," she told him, "my mother uses them both on me from time to time."

"I mean it. Stay out of it," he warned. She pouted. He frowned.

"Okay, okay," she said putting up her hands in fake surrender. "I won't do anything." She giggled so he didn't quite believe her. His frown got deeper. It made her shiver.

"I promise," she said holding up her hand in a "scout's honor salute". He was looking straight ahead and she leaned to catch his eye. She tilted her head more with her two fingers still on her forehead. He looked out of the corner of his eye.

"I don't think you're doing that right." He told her, referring to her salute.

"Well, I haven't been a Girl Scout in years. Friends?" she asked offering her hand for a handshake.

Anderson laughed and shook her hand. "Friends," he told her, but the moment their hands touched again he knew he would soon be aiming for more than mere friendship.

Anderson got out of the car when they reached City Line Avenue. The window had been rolled down and Anderson was saying good-bye. Gabrielle had moved closer to the door when he got out. Anderson reached through the window and touched her cheek with his index finger. Remembering where she was going to be very shortly, Anderson looked at her with concern. He fought against all the things he wanted to say. Gabrielle saw his jaw tighten and then he forced himself to smile at her. Her eyelids fluttered for a second before Gabrielle closed her eyes to hold back the tears. *What was it about this man that shook her to the very core?* She didn't…couldn't open her eyes right away.

"Stay safe, Gigi," he said. His voice was low, barely above a whisper and strained. He straightened, turned and walked away.

Gabrielle did not roll up the window right away. His words kept playing over in her mind. This was the second time he had said those two words. With just two words, this man without knowing it had re-charted the direction of her future. She knew full well that he was not responsible for her life but he was one of the reasons that she was starting to rethink a few things in it.

Yes, Anderson Ray was one of the reasons she was thinking about her future and a woman named Ruby was another. A single tear rolled down her face. She wiped away the tear with the back of her hand and rolled up the window.

Nathan had rolled down the partition when Anderson got out of the car. He observed the woman in the back seat. He recognized pain when he saw it. Besides, he'd seen this pain before, many times on his sister Ruby's face. He gave her a few minutes before he pressed the intercom's button. Gabrielle picked up the receiver.

"Yes?" Her voice was shaky…hesitant.

"Whenever you're ready?" Nathan told her in a tone that was warm and compassionate.

"Oh yes. Of course." She was beginning to compose herself.

Nathan eased the car away from the curb. He pressed the button again. Gabrielle picked up the receiver but she did not speak.

"It usually helps when I know **where** I'm going," he told her.

Gabrielle looked up. She could only see his eyes reflected in the rearview mirror but she knew he was smiling and it was infectious. She smiled back. She even laughed a little.

"Sorry. University City, please. Forty-eighth and Locust Street." He saw her face take on a somber expression after she answered him.

"Gabrielle?" Nathan called her name when he noticed that she had not hung up the receiver yet.

"Yes?" When she looked up, her expression was childlike, trusting. Her eyes were wide with surprise as if she was not expecting to hear her name again.

Nathan raised his eyes upward for a second. She was young enough to be his daughter and he was moved with fatherly concern.

"In the top drawer of the center compartment are some of our business cards. Take one or two. You call us if you ever need us."

She found the cards and took two of them. She put one in her purse and the other in her jacket pocket.

"I mean it," Nathan said again taking a parental tone. "If you **ever need us**, please call. Use the pager number. Code in your number and 9-1-1, we'll probably respond faster than the police." He smiled at her again.

"But that won't be nec..." She started to protest too quickly and she knew it. She stopped. After a few moments, she just nodded.

"That's a girl...And thanks for trusting us."

Not too long after Gabrielle gave Nathan her address, he pulled up in front of her apartment complex. He got out and opened the door for her. When she got out of the limo, Jimmy came running from the apartment. He looked like he could spit nails. The front of his maroon shirt was hanging out and unbuttoned and his feet were bare.

Jimmy thought that the man helping Gabrielle from the limousine was Anderson. He was ready for a fight this time. He wanted to amend the results of their last meeting. When Nathan straightened and turned around, Jimmy stopped running. The scene looked like a confrontation between a football fullback and a track runner. Nathan's eyes narrowed. He looked at Jimmy hard. What he saw was raw anger and it increased his own. He knew Jimmy wanted to lash out at Gabrielle...or him.

Not today, home. Nathan thought. *Today, **you** will know what it's like to **be** scared.*

Gabrielle was standing between Jimmy and Nathan who had just closed the car door. Nathan artfully maneuvered his way between Gabrielle and Jimmy.

"So Gabrielle, who's this young man, a friend of yours?"

"Uh yeah. Nathan Sharpe, Jimmy Rivers."

Oh yeah, so now, I got your last name you little weasel. Nathan thought to himself. The two men exchanged a strained handshake. Nathan held onto Jimmy's hand even when Jimmy tried to pull away.

"Well Gabrielle, listen, I really enjoyed helping out during this week of Career Month. Be sure to call me or Air if you should need us again." Gabrielle nodded.

"So Jimmy, my man," Nathan said placing his other hand on Jimmy's shoulder a little too firmly, "what kind of work do you do?" Nathan was talking and moving a lot so Jimmy could not pull away. He fired so many questions at Jimmy so fast; Jimmy was having trouble answering. Nathan was also trying to make sure Gabrielle could not figure out what he was doing.

Since she did not suspect that anything was amiss, Gabrielle headed for the apartment. When she was out of earshot, Nathan tightened his grip. Jimmy winced.

"Hey man, what's **your** problem?" Jimmy asked when Nathan finally released his hand.

"You...**you** are my problem," Nathan told him. He pointed his finger and connected with Jimmy's chest twice.

"Hey yo, I don't even know you."

"Yes you do," Nathan told him with eyes cold as ice. "I'm your worst nightmare!"

"Whatever is buggin' you, I'm not the one okay?" Jimmy said shaking his hand to try and restore some feeling in it. He was afraid of this man and he did not like being afraid, not one bit. Nathan stared at him so hard, Jimmy backed up to the limo.

Nathan was so close to him; Jimmy could feel his breath. Nathan leaned over him. His eyes seemed to bore a hole right through Jimmy.

"Maybe I can't stop Gabrielle from living with you, but I can make life really miserable for you if you lay one hand on her."

Jimmy swallowed but he tried to bluff his way through by chuckling.

"Hey man, that's **my** woman and I mean, you know how they can get sometimes. You know, sometimes they make you mad and..."

"And what?" Nathan asked, his tone threatening. "Brothahs like you make me sick! **Men** like you make me sick and it ain't even about color! Tell you what, fool...next time she makes you mad enough to pound something; you can come see me. We can go a few rounds if your heart can stand it. I guarantee you, I'll be more of a challenge than some woman."

Nathan pointed his finger at Jimmy's chest again connecting with the spot where Jimmy's heart was racing. Nathan straightened up to his full height and folded his arms across his chest. He was still standing very close to Jimmy. Jimmy was clearly shaken. He was still leaning with his elbows resting on the limo to support himself. Nathan walked around the limousine to the driver's side. Jimmy stood up. Nathan looked at Jimmy over the hood of the car.

"You touch her and I'll be on you like a second layer of skin," Nathan warned in a menacing tone. "Do you catch my drift, son?"

"Jimmy!" Nathan called again. Jimmy stiffened.

"Yeah, all right already. I got it. I got it," Jimmy said walking away.

When Nathan got in the car, he pressed the accelerator too hard. The speed of the car clearly reflected his anger. He applied the brakes gently. *I'm sorry, baby*, he thought as if speaking to the car, *no need taking it out on you*. He let out a breath slowly and turned on the radio. He needed to calm down.

His temples were throbbing. It wasn't exactly a headache but this stress could bring one.

Seeing Jimmy had made him angrier than he had anticipated. He was too much like Adam and everything with Ruby had flashed back to Nathan's mind. When he spied Jimmy running toward them and the look in his eyes, Nathan had prepared for the young punk. When Jimmy slowed down, Nathan recognized him from the videotape of the break-in at the office. He still had to find out what that was all about, but now that the office was secure again, he had nothing but time.

Nathan shook his head as if to clear it. He needed a distraction. Something that would take his thoughts in a more pleasant direction would be quite welcome now. Something or **someone.** Nathan turned up the volume on the radio as Mariah Carey sang "Got To Be Real." He sang along as the song played and made a hard left toward Mt. Airy Circle.

CHAPTER IX

By the time Jimmy came into the apartment, Gabrielle had changed into a tee shirt and shorts. Jazz was coming from the radio in the kitchen and she had pulled ground beef from the freezer to prepare with some stir-fry vegetables. Jimmy slammed the front door. Gabrielle jumped but she did not enter the living room. Their apartment was Y-shaped with three rooms and a bath. Their living room was between the kitchen and the bedroom. The dining area was near the living room picture window across the room from the front door. All the rooms were painted the typical off-white for apartments so; Gabrielle had added colorful accessories to each room.

She decided to wait and see if Jimmy wanted to say anything but he flopped down on the loveseat in front of the television. He turned the volume on the TV set up loud. Whenever Gabrielle would ask him to turn it down an argument would ensue, so she decided to leave him alone this time. She had looked out of the living room window once and saw Nathan leaning over Jimmy. Gabrielle was curious about what had been said but she was not going to ask. She prepared a pitcher of lemonade and placed it on their little dinette table along with two glasses filled with ice cubes.

While the ground beef was thawing in the microwave, Gabrielle set the table. She turned to go back into the kitchen. In that brief moment, Jimmy caught her eye. He heard her intake of breath and he saw her fear. She had placed her splayed hand against her chest as if to slow her heart and she exhaled. Gabrielle saw something in his face too, but she was not quite sure what it was. Pain? Maybe even regret. Whatever it was, Jimmy was not talking. He was wrestling with some inner demon but he was not telling her anything.

He looked at her for a moment longer and then mumbled something about not being hungry. Gabrielle went to the kitchen to finish preparing dinner as Jimmy was putting on his shoes. A few minutes later, she heard Jimmy leave. She did not know what transpired between Jimmy and Nathan but Jimmy was clearly not himself. Oddly enough, Gabrielle was relieved. Tonight when she went to bed, she would get a good night's sleep. She was sure of it.

Anderson was a bit more cautious when he went to the office that afternoon. He had already concluded that the person who broke into the office would not return any time soon but he was not about to take chances. He could not afford to be careless. The one time in his life when he had been, his partner got hurt. That was another reason he'd left the police force. He had been too much of a hot shot and he realized that acting like a Dirty Harry only worked in the movies.

The office was undisturbed. Anderson breathed a sigh of relief. Thanks to Nathan, the office was more secure. Thanks to Nathan, all the information he had gathered on his mother was still intact. Anderson smiled as his eyes went to the 8x10 photo on his desk. He had insisted on the photo when their two skills combined and they changed the name of the company. Anderson looked at the picture of him standing side by side with Nathan in their official uniforms. They only wore the uniforms for special events. They still did their best work undercover.

He was still staring at the picture when his thoughts became personal. Anderson fully understood why this man had been his father's best friend. They had had so much in common. It was no wonder that he and Nathan worked so well together. Sometimes, they even thought alike.

The ringing of the telephone interrupted his thoughts.

"Rayzor-Sharpe, Ray here."

First, he heard static and then a voice spoke. "The wisest thing for you to do is leave well enough alone. People might be hurt if you don't. Leave this alone," the voice told him.

Anderson listened for a moment longer. He heard a tape recorder click. He tried to detect other noises. Within a few seconds, the line went dead. Anderson hung up. He went to the special voice modulator Nathan had connected to the phone system. Every incoming call was recorded whether it went through the answering machine or not. Anderson replayed the tape. It was a female voice that had been purposely distorted. For a moment, Anderson wondered if it had been the voice of his mother. He felt no kinship to the voice, no tug at his heart. Instead, the words gave him a chill. This is bigger than a simple missing person, he thought. Something is very wrong.

Nathan changed his mind about driving the limo to Brandeis's house. He parked it in the garage near the office and took his Durango instead. He left the uniform jacket in the limousine and changed to his navy blue Polo jacket. Nathan debated stopping by the office to see if Anderson was okay but he decided to go to his original destination. If his godson needed anything he had his cell phone number.

When Nathan arrived at Brandeis's house he heard music. He was standing on the porch waiting for her to answer the door. He had rung the bell but she had not yet answered. The music was not really loud, at least not loud enough to be unpleasant but he suspected that she had not heard the bell. He walked over to the picture window to knock and the sight that he saw took his breath away. Brandeis was dancing. She was alternating between African, modern dance and Caribbean. Nathan recognized some of her steps. She was wearing a one piece, purple tights set and flowing white wrap skirt. She looked *like an angel in flight*, he thought. He watched her until the song ended. Then, he went back to the front door. He did not want the neighbors to report him as a Peeping Tom. Since there was a lull in the music, Nathan took the opportunity to ring the doorbell again. Brandeis was changing the CD.

Brandeis answered the door, sweaty and out of breath. She had a towel draped over her shoulders. As she opened the door, her eyes widened and then she smiled.

"Hello, tall, dark and tired," she said doing her best Mae West impression, including a hand on her hip.

Nathan shook his head, laughing. She was like a breath of fresh air. He had begun to feel better long before she answered the door. He took a step back and looked at her from head to toes. She was barefoot. He raised an eyebrow in appreciation. Nathan had a thing for feet. Brandeis had cute, small feet.

When Brandeis saw where Nathan was looking, she wriggled her toes.

"You gonna let 'em get cold or are you coming in?" she asked feeling the draft from the cool evening air. Nathan shrugged.

Without another word, he grabbed her around the waist, picked her up and stepped inside the house. In fluid movements, he shut the door, locked it and carried her into the living room where he placed her gently on her feet on the carpeted floor.

Brandeis put her hands on her hips and looked at him. Then she threw back her head and laughed. "That's what I like, a take-charge kinda-man," she teased.

"Then you'll love me. I'm **real** pushy," Nathan shot back smiling.

"Would you like some coffee?" she asked. She sensed that something was wrong.

"If you don't mind," Nathan began, "I'd rather have some of that herbal tea you drink."

Brandeis smiled and sashayed toward the kitchen with a lot of emphasis in her walk.

"Now, cut that out!" Nathan scolded as he watched her walk away.

"Sorry...can't help it. It's built in, Honey." she called to him over her shoulder.

Nathan shook his head and laughed again. This was exactly what he needed. The tension, the stress and the threatening headache were already subsiding. He took off his jacket and placed it on a chair. He took a seat on the sofa.

Brandeis paused in the dining room doorway. She stopped to look at the big man sitting in her living room. Strange, she should have been self-conscious about her weight and her height around him but Nathan did not make her feel small or uncomfortable. He had come by because he wanted to see her. He had sought her out. She felt special. She dropped her eyes to the tray she was carrying. She felt good. A man had not made her feel this way in a long time. She had not let a man get this close in ages. Brandeis was so engrossed in her thoughts, she was not even aware that Nathan was now looking at her intently.

Nathan studied Brandeis. He watched her facial expressions. They changed several times. He saw her go from sly and sensual to sweet and sentimental. *Men who didn't take the time to study women were such fools*, he thought. *"Fools!"* The word flashed out before him and his dark thought turned to Jimmy. He frowned so hard his nostrils flared. He shook his head and sucked in his breath. At the same moment, he heard cups rattle.

Brandeis had been observing him the whole time. She watched him go through changes she did not understand. She had looked down for a second or two but then when she looked up he was angry. Something had suddenly made him very angry.

Swiftly, Nathan sprang to his feet and went to her. He grabbed the tray from Brandeis with one hand and took hold of her hand with the other and guided her into the living room. Her hand felt tense and he knew he had caused it. He set the tray on the coffee table in front of the sofa. Brandeis sat down. Nathan joined her. He stroked her knuckles gently with his thumb. Her eyes were down cast. He kept up his mini-massage until she looked at him. Her gaze went to the tray. She had fixed two mugs of Red Zinger tea. His mug was larger than hers. She had also popped some popcorn in the microwave. Nathan took his finger and placed it under her chin. When she turned to face him, he smiled revealing those deep, adorable dimples. Brandeis smiled back. Then she cleared her throat.

"I thought we'd watch a video," she told him breaking the silence. She went to dim the lights.

"That sounds like a winner. Which one?" he asked settling back comfortably on the sofa. Brandeis joined him.

"Soul Food."

"Good choice. I liked that movie," Nathan said stretching his arm across the back of the sofa.

"Me too," she said moving closer to that arm.

Soon they were sitting close together on the sofa. Nathan's arm was around her shoulder. Brandeis heard Nathan blow out a deep breath and she turned to look at him.

"I met Jimmy today," he told her frowning.

CHAPTER X

Cassandra Rivers paced the floor of her studio apartment. Her long brown hair was pulled tight in a ponytail that brushed her shoulders every time she turned her head toward the door. She was on her third cigarette. The light knock on the door had a special pattern so she knew exactly who it was.

"Get in here!" she shouted with anger punctuating every word.

Her visitor came in and took a seat in the recliner although he did not dare push it back. His feet were planted firmly on the floor. His elbows rested on his knees and his head was down. He had failed her and he knew she was not happy about it.

"You screwed up," she started in, her voice laced with irritation. "I told you to get me everything."

"I tried," he pleaded. "I brought you everything I could find."

"Then, **why** are they still looking?" she hissed. Her green eyes stared at the top of his head since his head was still down.

"I guess they had a back-up file somewhere else." He knew the moment he said it that it was the wrong answer to give her.

"Any dummy knows people keep back-up files. Why didn't you erase them or something? Some computer expert you are. What did I pay all that tuition for?" She stumped out her cigarette.

"To keep me out of the way," he yelled, his green eyes now reflecting the same gold flecks as hers when he was angry.

"Jimmy, you watch your mouth," she warned.

"Look Mom, I erased the hidden files coded 'Cassi' and I brought you everything from the paper trail I found. What more could I do? If I..." Jimmy shoved his fingers through his hair then tried to smooth the waves back in place.

"If you had not been in such a hurry to get back to that tramp girlfriend of yours, you would have had time," Cassandra lashed out at him.

"She's **not** a tramp, Mom. Why do you always do that?" He already knew what she would say.

"She's dark-skinned isn't she? They're all tramps! Dark-skinned people have always caused me nothing but trouble." Her beige complexion flared red and her voice wavered. Her eyes filled up with tears. She shook her head violently to ward off a crying spell.

Jimmy was confused. He never understood his mother's problem with people of darker hues. He knew she wasn't white. His grandfather was Latino and his grandmother was African-American. She told him that she had to change her name from Rivera to Rivers when she started her modeling career. He even knew about the Italian guy that fathered him but his mother had other secrets. Secrets that made her abandon her own people.

"Mom," he began softly, "I'll find out what's going on. I promise. But maybe the tape you had me make for you will scare them off."

"Jimmy, do you honestly think those two will be chased off by a lousy taped message?"

Jimmy hated when she was like this. The more he tried to reason with her, the more unreasonable she became. When she stopped pacing, she threw herself into a chair and crossed her legs. She lit another cigarette. She was staring straight ahead. She took a long drag, held the smoke for a few moments and blew it out in an exasperated breath.

Jimmy got up to leave. Slowly he made his way to the door. He did not know what else he could say to her. He loved her and he could not bear it when he disappointed her. After all, she had done everything for him all his life. He put his hand on the doorknob and paused.

"Mom, is that guy Anderson really...my brother?" He opened the door.

"**Half**-brother," she corrected. Cassandra inhaled deeply and blew the smoke out. She never looked in his direction and Jimmy closed the door quietly behind him.

By Friday morning, Gabrielle had had more than thirty-six hours to herself. Jimmy had not come back since Wednesday night. Gabrielle could see that his confrontation with Nathan had shook him up. He did not return that night and there were no signs that he had been to the apartment at all on Thursday. Gabrielle had plenty of time to do some serious thinking. She had gotten two good nights of sleep and thought about the woman she had seen on the television. On Thursday, after work she had even called the hotline for Women Against Abuse and gotten some information. She woke up an hour early on Friday and even while she was still in her pajamas, she started packing. She wanted to start while her mind was made up and before she started making excuses for Jimmy. She knew if she thought about it too hard, she would change her mind by justifying his behavior again. She had not totally unpacked when she returned from the conference so filling up another suitcase or two was easy. She was not going to take any furniture since most of it belonged to Jimmy. There was no point in making him angrier. He would be unpredictable when he realized that she was gone. It would get worse once he realized that she was gone for good. She also decided not to clean out the bureau drawers until she got home that afternoon. She did not want to arose suspicion in case he came home in the middle of the afternoon. She shoved the suitcases all the way back into the closet and got ready for work. She felt good as she showered. She had made some tough decisions but she was taking charge of her life. It was still **her** life. She dressed in a navy blue pants suit and yellow blouse and even took the time to put on a little make-up. She felt empowered and it was exhilarating. Before she left the house, she dialed the number on the business card she had put in her pocketbook.

"Rayzor-Sharpe."

"Mr. Sharpe?" Gabrielle's voice was crisp, definite.

"No, no, no," he chastised gently. But Gabrielle was sure she recognized Nathan's voice. She closed her eyes with realization.

"Nathan," she said with more familiar tone.

"At your service," his voice was reassuring. Once again, she heard a fatherly tone in it, "What can I do for you?"

"Today is moving day!" she declared.

"Good Girl!" Nathan said praising her decision, "What time?"

"About three o'clock. This is an early dismissal day." Gabrielle replied with more confidence than she realized.

"Does Jimmy know what time school lets out?"

"No. In fact, I haven't seen him since you brought me home. I have no idea where he is."

"Excellent. See you then," Nathan hung up.

Anderson was in his office looking over the file he had reconstructed on his mother. He had so much information but not one solid lead on where she was.

Cassandra Rivers was once one of the city's top paid models. Now, she was in hiding someplace. Anderson had no idea why. She had graduated from the same high school as Anderson's father, Clayton and Nathan Sharpe. She disappeared for about a year. Her diploma listed her name as Cassandria Rivera. Anderson figured that his mother left town to have her baby and returned long enough to surrender the baby (Anderson) to his father. She remained in the city for about two months and disappeared again. While away from people who knew her, Cassandria Rivera reinvented herself. She invested in a complete makeover. One year later, she emerged in Chicago as CaSandra Rivers.

She had gone from one hundred fifty pounds to one hundred pounds and her brown hair was blonde. After modeling in Chicago for some local dress designers, she moved to New York to further her career. In no time, she was in high demand and had her pick of modeling jobs where she was paid thousands of dollars per job.

CaSandra was a photographer's dream! She photographed well and posed even better. Her face appeared in pictures all over the city. A number of famous photographers and artists were snapping her picture or sketching her portrait. She even posed for a sculpture entitled "Madonna in Waiting" and the unknown sculptor became an overnight sensation. For that job alone, CaSandra was paid five thousand dollars.

The following year, CaSandra took Philadelphia by storm! Her picture graced many magazine ads and local billboards all over the city and young Anderson did not even realize who she was. On a regular basis, she could be seen on the cover of romance novels and even as a character in cartoons for a local newspaper. She was the model for a popular superhero in the new Ravel comic books and it's young readers weren't even aware that she was born and raised in Philadelphia.

Twenty years ago, when Anderson was ten years old, the media did a write-up about an expensive portrait painted by aspiring artist, Damien Andrez. The dazzling green eyes in the picture seem to follow their admirer all over the room. The portrait entitled "The Lonely Woman" sold at an auction for forty thousand dollars. Not long after that and for reasons unknown, CaSandra dropped out of sight again.

Anderson fingered the large manila envelope that had been delivered by registered mail. He had checked the return address. It was an abandoned house. There were three 9x12 glossy photos inside. Two were black and white, the last one was a color print. All of them were pictures of CaSandra. Anderson's heart was beating fast and hard against his chest. He stared at the eyes looking back at him. There was something written on the back of each picture. The first picture was "Cassandra now - age 47." The sender obviously ignored how CaSandra preferred to spell her name. Even though it was a black and white photo,

Anderson guessed the hair color to be brown. The second picture identified "Cassandra at age 30." This was the color picture. The ash blonde hair and beige complexion were an interesting contrast but CaSandra wore it well. The last photo in black and white was the most interesting. Cassandra at age 17." In this photograph, she was a dark-haired, pretty girl, a brunette.

Nathan had already told Anderson that CaSandra or Cassandria, as she was known back then, had very dark hair and alluring green eyes. She was full-figured. Her classmates probably called her "Chubby" or something just as bad, Anderson thought. Peers can be so insensitive.

Looking at the last photo, Anderson could understand why his dad had been crazy about her. She had a baby fine face and gorgeous eyes!

Pain hit Anderson's chest hard but it was not physical. He had seen those eyes and that face all over the city, yet he never knew that the face looking back at him was his mother. Anderson was still looking at the picture when Nathan walked into the office. He had been on the phone after completing some morning work and checking on information about Jimmy. Nathan had called Anderson's name twice before the younger man looked up. Nathan saw pain in his eyes before Anderson looked away. Nathan frowned. Something had upset his godson. He walked over to the desk and looked at the photo in Anderson's hands. Nathan's chest tightened. It had been a long time since he'd seen those eyes. What had his friend, Clay called them? "Haunting."

"So this is what she looked like in school," Anderson replied needing to break the silence.

"Yeah, we didn't have a yearbook picture when you started to search for her. She had refused to take one," Nathan told him. "She thought her class thought she was ugly. Some of the dark-skinned girls called her some pretty ugly names. Some of the students were pretty cruel just because she was overweight. She went home in tears a lot." Nathan paused as if remembering something.

"But not Clay. He really loved her, Air. Your dad **really** loved her." Nathan's voice wavered a little. He got up and left the room.

Anderson was puzzled. Nathan never behaved like that before. *Like what before?* Anderson was not sure how to describe Nathan's behavior.

"Hey-y-y, wait a minute," Nathan said suddenly from the outer office. He went to his desk and quickly opened the folder he had received from the police. He took a picture from the pile of information and re-entered Anderson's office. Nathan placed the photo of Jimmy, age twenty-two, next to the one of Cassandra at age seventeen. The resemblance was unmistakable.

"Well, what have we here?" Anderson looked on in amazement. It changed to disbelief. He was clearly shaken by this revelation.

"Ladies and gentlemen, we have a match," Nathan said out loud.

Anderson rolled his swivel chair away from the desk and looked out the window. He had a beautiful view of City Line Avenue. He did not even notice. Confusion was clouding his vision. He was wrestling with pain, hurt, and surprise.

"Oh my God," he sighed and shut his eyes but his eyelids were soon warm and moist.

Nathan put his hand on Anderson's shoulder. Anderson drew in a breath as he sat straight up in his chair. Silent tears rolled down his face. He swiped at them with the back of his hand.

"Do you know what this means, Nate? Do you realize that I…" Anderson's voice faded into a muffled sob.

"Well son, it looks like you have a **half-brother**."

"Yeah," Anderson tensed. "A half-brother who abuses women." His jaw tightened.

"True, but Air, I think there's still a silver lining to this dark cloud."

"Really? What?"

"Gabrielle called this morning," Nathan told him.

Anderson raised an eyebrow. He turned his head to look at his mentor.

"Today is moving day," Nathan said with emphasis on moving!

"Hallelujah!" Anderson said raising his arms. He gave Nathan a high five and smiled for the first time all day.

CHAPTER XI

It was a smooth, easy, school day, even though it was a Friday. At three o'clock Nathan's Durango and Anderson's Pathfinder pulled up in front of Gabrielle's apartment. Gabrielle was packed and waiting. There were only a few boxes with her suitcases. Anderson went up to the apartment with Gabrielle. Not only did she look very nice in her pantsuit, she seemed positively energized. Nathan looked around outside and then he joined them in the apartment. The three of them moved swiftly. Nathan had a hand truck and a luggage carrier which made their job easy. Gabrielle had not packed anything really heavy so the three of them were able to move her things in one trip. They placed most of her belongings in Nathan's Durango. Gabrielle rode with Anderson.

Nathan sped off as soon as everything was in his van. Anderson did not drive off right away. He turned to Gabrielle and gave her an encouraging smile. She dropped her eyes when she felt her cheeks flush. "I'm proud of you." Anderson took hold of her hand.

"I'm proud of me too," Gabrielle told him affirmatively. "I should have done this a while ago." She was not really talking to him but she did need to say it out loud. She held his hand a little while longer.

"You're doing it now," he said giving her hand a gentle squeeze, "that's all that matters."

As Anderson pulled away from the curb, Gabrielle instinctively looked over her shoulder toward the apartment. Anderson glanced at her with concern.

"Gabrielle." He spoke her name softly and with affection.

They had stopped for a traffic light and he took the opportunity to look at her. He saw the tears beginning to form. He knew she was torn. He also knew this was a hard step for her but very necessary. He spoke to her with understanding in his voice.

"Gabrielle, **that** was your past. This is the first step toward your future. Please, don't be afraid. There is no reason to regret the decision you've made," he assured her. He turned his attention back to traffic as the light changed.

"You're right and I know that," she answered with a half smile. "I should start to concentrate on my future."

Easing through traffic, both of them were silent for a while. Anderson turned on the radio at a low volume and the mellow tunes on the radio helped ease the mood. Anderson reached across to touch her hand if her expression showed sadness. She would occasionally give him a half smile and lower her eyes. She was trying hard to remain determined and Anderson was showing as much support as he could. One thing he had learned in his profession was patience. He would give her as much time as she needed. If she needed someone to talk to, he would be close.

Whenever she was sure he was watching the road, Gabrielle would glance over at him. He seemed so sure of himself, so in control. She especially liked watching his hands as he drove the car. He had strong, powerful hands. She had already seen a demonstration of their force and his control. She knew he pulled his punch with Jimmy. Jimmy, he was so impetuous and quick tempered. At one time, Gabrielle thought that those actions were cute. Now, she was not sure how she formed such a notion. Jimmy was immature. Gabrielle knew that now. She had been doing a lot of thinking during their relationship but had refused to face certain things for a good while.

After watching the television program, she had called several places that dealt with abusive relationships. One of the counselors had helped her see just how childish and dangerous Jimmy's behavior was. She told Gabrielle that women often believe that they can change the man; *if they just love him enough* but these kinds of men need help, professional help and "loves got nothin' to do with it." After taking a more objective view of their six months together, she was glad she was walking away. She was relieved that she was **able** to walk away. She stole a glance in Anderson's direction again. He smiled at her before turning his attention back to the traffic.

"Uh…Anderson," she said his name softly.

"Hmmm?" He was looking straight ahead.

"Will you…?"

"Will I what?" he asked curiously.

"Will you be around to be part of that future we were just talking about?" She asked the question with hesitancy. She didn't want to move too fast especially since she had just decided to discontinue a relationship. She wanted to be sure of herself. She would have to be sure of what she wanted, from now on.

They had stopped for a light so Anderson took the opportunity to turn to her. He took her left hand and placed a feather-like kiss on her knuckles. "I won't lie to you, Gigi. I do want to be part of your future, a very big part. I've thought about you a lot since the first moment I saw you. I wasn't going to do anything as long as Jimmy was in the picture. I'll give you all the space you need, but as soon as you say…"

Someone behind them honked their horn. Anderson and Gabrielle noticed that the light had changed. He smiled and she blushed.

As they moved along the streets, Gabrielle noticed that they were in Willow Grove. Gabrielle frowned. "Air," she said using his nickname for the first time. "Where are you taking me?"

"I've been meaning to talk to you about that," Anderson told her as he pulled the Pathfinder into a restaurant parking lot.

"I think you know that Jimmy is not going to go away peacefully, Gigi." Anderson began as he turned to face her. "Nate and I have been talking. There are some things you don't know yet, but I'm sure they will make Jimmy twice as mad that you left right now. I promise to sit down and share all of that with you soon but right now, my main concern is your safety."

Gabrielle was confused but for the moment, she was content that Anderson wanted them to stop to get something to eat. They went into the restaurant together and sat at a booth.

After the waiter came and took their order, Anderson began to elaborate on what he had said earlier. "Jimmy will be highly upset when he realizes that you don't plan to return. But there are some other things you need to know. I'm sure they'll set him off when he connects the dots…as I have." Anderson sighed, out loud and Gabrielle knew there was more.

"For the last three years, I've been searching for my mother. Recently, I uncovered some information that let me know she's in the city and that's not all. Someone broke into the office earlier in the week and stole the records."

"Oh Air." Gabrielle's voice was sympathetic.

"It's okay," he assured her. "Thanks to Nathan, a lot of information had been saved in a back-up file. Gigi, I discovered something earlier today that…"

Anderson hesitated. He did not want to hurt her. Even though Gabrielle had moved out and literally left her relationship with Jimmy behind her, Anderson knew that you don't turn feelings on and off that quickly.

"What is it, Air? Tell me. Please." Gabrielle reached across the table and touched his arm but the waiter came with their orders so she had to move her hand. She put it back as soon as the waiter left them. "Please, tell me. If you think I need to know, tell me."

"It involves the videotape of the break-in. The guy who stole the files had a lot of computer smarts."

Gabrielle's intake of breath was audible and Anderson could tell by the way her eyes widened that she had guessed what he was going to say. "Air, you don't mean…?"

"It was Jimmy. I couldn't believe it myself but we intensified the images on the surveillance tape and positively identified him."

"But, why?" Gabrielle asked. She was clearly confused by what Anderson was telling her.

Anderson paused. He took a sip of his soda and setting the glass down he reached for her hand. He looked at her intently before he went back to what he started to tell her earlier. "Gigi, some information I got earlier today indicates…It seems that Jimmy, well, he could be my," he swallowed, "my half-brother."

"Oh no! Your half-brother? Are you serious?" She paused as she tried to take in what he had told her. "What are you going to do? Wait. Air, are you sure? Maybe it's a mistake."

Anderson shook his head. "I doubt it, Gigi. From everything I can confirm, Jimmy and I have the same mother."

Gabrielle looked stunned. She sat straight up in her seat and blinked her eyes. She decided to try and eat something. They both did. The problem was, they were both too preoccupied with what Anderson had just said. There was a dull silence between them. They continued to eat their meal. Neither of them knew what to say to the other. After they both had eaten half of their meal, Gabrielle could not stand the quiet any longer.

"Air, what are you going to do?"

"I don't know. Right now, I'm more concerned about you. Jimmy will be dangerous now. Dangerous to both of us. When he discovers that you actually moved out, he will be like a time bomb. Once he realizes that we're brothers and if he believes that you're with me, that will just make matters worse. I've seen this kind of thing before. He's already a powder-keg so, there's no telling what he'll do. I just want you safe, Gigi. You'll have to be very careful; very careful for a while." Anderson paused and reached for her hand. "Men like Jimmy are shrewd. He'll probably be very penitent at first. He could sound pretty persuasive…"

Gabrielle held up her hand. She locked gaze with Anderson. "My mind is made up. It was time to leave so I left." Anderson nodded with understanding.

He heard the determination in her voice. The couple finished their meal in silence and after Anderson left a sizable tip on the table, they left the restaurant.

CHAPTER XII

When Jimmy opened the apartment door, he knew something was not right. All the furniture was there but something was missing. The kitchen was spotless. All the little strawberry accessories that Gabrielle had added were still there but untouched. It was as if no one had been in the kitchen. Jimmy went into the bedroom. Everything was intact. The bed was made; the room was neat. Yet, something was wrong. Jimmy raked his fingers though his hair and then he saw it—the big empty space on the dresser where Gabrielle's cosmetics used to be. There was nothing there. He checked the drawers - empty. He went to her closet - empty. He ran back in the living room. Even the CDs she'd bought were gone. Jimmy felt empty all the way to the pit of his stomach. Then he panicked. He ran all through the apartment as if the first time had been a bad dream but it was true. She was gone! He flung himself down on the sofa. Then he saw something on the floor—business card.

"Rayzor-Sharpe Security and Private Investigations?" Jimmy said out loud. Suddenly, he was furious. "It's bad enough I find out you're my brother. Now you try to take **my** woman. Well-l-l," he began, his anger mounting, "I don't think so, Big Bro.' I don't think so!" Jimmy got up from the sofa. He shoved the business card in his pocket and walked out of the apartment, slamming the door behind him.

Jimmy drove so fast he almost had two accidents with other cars. He drove straight to Brandeis's house. Once he was on the porch, he pounded on the door.

Brandeis looked at the clock in her living room. It was six in the evening. When she went into the vestibule, she saw Jimmy on the other side of the door. Brandeis saw the fury on his face. She did not open the door. Instead, she met his anger with annoyance.

"What do **you** want? I was eating my dinner."

"Don't you play dumb with me, woman. Where is she?"

"Where's who?" she retorted. She stared at him.

The man looking back at her was raging, his nostrils flaring. He was breathing heavily; his hair was a mess. He looked haggard.

All of a sudden, Brandeis threw her hands on her hips, flung her head back and laughed out loud. "I don't believe it!" She said. "She left your sorry butt didn't she?" Brandeis looked at him, amusement showed all over her face.

"Gigi finally did it! Ah-ha-ha. Oh this is precious," She taunted again, "she packed up and left; so, you came running over here." She didn't even try to hide how pleased she was.

"Sorry, sugah," she said sarcastically, "but my baby ain't here. See Jimmy, she's smart. She probably figured you'd come charging over here first and decided to go some place where you **can't** get at her."

Jimmy grabbed the handle on the screen door and shook it violently. Brandeis jumped back. She was grateful that the screen door **and** the front door were locked.

"Where is she?" he yelled as he rattled the door.

Brandeis backed away from the door slowly.

Jimmy was so angry he did not notice what she was doing. She closed the vestibule door quietly and picked up the phone. She dialed a number. When she hung up she went back to the door. Jimmy was still standing on the porch.

"Jimmy," she said as calmly as she could, "please, go away. If you don't leave the police…"

"Police," he yelled, "don't talk to me about police. Just tell me where Gabby is. All I want is my woman."

"She's not your property, Jimmy and if she's really left you, she doesn't want to be with you anymore, or at least, not right now." Brandeis stated flatly. She tried to keep her voice calm and not agitate him any more than he was. "I'm sure that if Gigi wants to talk to you she'll…"

"Shut up!" he said, slamming his fist against the wooden part of the door. "She loves me. Do you hear that, old woman?" he yelled as he stomped around on the porch.

"She **did** love you, yes; but Jimmy, maybe, she finally loves herself more," Brandeis said proudly but trying not to gloat.

"It's that Anderson guy," Jimmy said snarling, "he stole her."

"Jimmy, listen to yourself. Get real. People can't steal people." Brandeis replied. She gave up trying to reason with him. "If she left, she did it because she wanted to. You sent her away by abusing her."

"No. I told you to shut-up." Jimmy shouted, "He did this. He took her."

"Oh pah-leeze, Jimmy. She left because she was fed up. I warned you that you might lose her. You wouldn't listen. Now, look what's happened."

Jimmy grabbed at the door again but he was distracted by a horn that suddenly blasted behind him. He grabbed at the door once more and the horn sounded again several times.

Brandeis smiled when she saw the Durango pull up in front of her door.

"I think you'd better go," she told Jimmy sternly.

Jimmy looked around. He looked toward the street. He did not know who was in the SUV with the tinted windows but it made him uncomfortable and Brandeis was looking very smug. He reached for the door handle one more time and again, the horn blasted. Jimmy was finally convinced that it was not a coincidence. Jimmy hurriedly stepped off the porch. He got in his car and drove away. The Durango followed him for at least ten blocks and then pulled away.

Brandeis breathed a sigh of relief and closed her vestibule door. The phone rang and she practically ran to answer it.

"Hi Ma-Dear," Gabrielle said once Brandeis picked up the phone.

"Gigi, baby, where are you? That fool was here acting like a madman. Are you okay? Is Anderson with you?" Brandeis was firing off questions faster than Gabrielle could answer them.

"Mom, slow down. I'm fine," Gabrielle told her once she could get a word in to answer. "No, Anderson is not with me, not now anyway but yes, I was with him earlier."

"I'll be by to go to church with you Sunday and we'll spend the whole day together okay? I promise I'll tell you everything then. But for now, I'll say this - I'm not going back to Jimmy, Mom. I've left for good. I'd tell you where I am but Jimmy might come back but don't worry, Ma-Dear, I'm safe."

"That's good, Baby. I'll sleep better knowing you're safe. And Gigi?"

"Yes, Ma-Dear?"

"I love you."

"I love you too, Mom. See you Sunday." They both hung up the phones.

Gabrielle was watching television when she heard a motor outside. It stopped and she listened as a vehicle alarm was set. Then, she heard the front door close. She heard keys jingling and a few minutes later Nathan walked into the living room. He put his keys on an end table and took a seat in his burgundy recliner.

"Is my mom really okay?" she asked him, turning off the T.V.

"Oh yeah, she's just fine," he assured her smiling.

"Thanks for checking on her," Gabrielle told him gratefully.

"No need to thank me," he told her as he eased back in his recliner. "I was glad she paged me. I wasn't that far away when she called. When she put in the 9-1-1 code after her number, I figured I should go by there instead of calling."

"I bet Jimmy was really upset to see you," Gabrielle replied almost asking a question.

"Not really. He didn't **see** me," Nathan informed her. "All he saw was a big, black machine honking it's horn at him. I never got out. I think that rattled his nerves even more. He hurried off the porch, got in his car and took off like a rabbit.

"Oh Nathan. I bet he was so nervous he could hardly start the car."

"Something like that," Nathan said with a smirk on his face. "But if he wasn't nervous when he got in the car, he certainly was when I followed him."

"You followed him?"

"Oh yeah, for about ten blocks," Nathan told her folding his arms and looking smug. "I wanted to make sure he got the point. I think it worked. If nothing else, I shook him up pretty good. I don't think he'll be bothering your mother for a while."

He eased back in the recliner and Gabrielle heard him let out a tired groan.

"Nathan."

He sat up straight as soon as he heard his name. He relaxed when he realized Gabrielle was still in the room.

"Sorry," he said sheepishly. "I'm not used to anyone being here but Smoke and me."

"Smoke? Nathan, I've been here three hours and I haven't seen anyone."

Just then, they heard a noise in the kitchen.

"**That** would be Smoke," he told her as he looked at his watch. "He's early so he might go back out again. He's such a player."

Gabrielle raised her eyebrows and her eyes widened as the biggest gray cat she had even seen sauntered into the room, climbed up on Nathan's lap and curled up. "See," he said smiling, "Smoke!"

"She...I mean 'He'..." she amended when Nathan shook his head, "really **does** look like a puff of smoke."

"A **very big,** puff..." Nathan gestured the cat's size with both hands, "of smoke." He smiled at the cat as Smoke raised his head. The cat looked at each one of them and settled back down on his master's lap.

"Oh my, yes," Gabrielle gestured too. "What kind of cat is he?"

"Smoke is a Maine-coon. I got him when I was in New England on an assignment. They are considered to be the only Native American cats in this country. Considering my heritage, when I found that out, it just seemed natural for him to come home with me."

"Well, Smoke is definitely the biggest cat I've ever seen."

Nathan wiggled his eyebrows. "Humph, some people say that about **me** too."

Gabrielle put her hand over her mouth and laughed out loud.

Nathan was dozing off while absent-mindedly stroking the cat, so she decided to call it a night too.

"Nathan," Gabrielle called softly.

"Hmmm?" Nathan said opening his eyes slowly.

"Thanks for letting me stay here," she told him smiling.

"Air and I talked about it. We both wanted to make sure you'd be safe...**and** I wanted your mom to be at ease about **where** you were." Gabrielle nodded and smiled as she caught his other meaning.

"Oh, I'm sure she is now and once, I talk to her on Sunday, I don't think she'll worry anymore. We're going to church together," she informed him.

"I know."

"You do?"

"Yep. I'm going too," he said casually.

"Nathan, that's not really necessary. I'll be fine," she assured him.

"I know," he said matter-of-factly. "but that's only **one** reason I'm going." Then he gave her a big grin.

Gabrielle suddenly got a big grin of her own and her eyes widened. "Oh my - you **really do** like my mother, don't you?"

"I do." He closed he eyes with a nod and feigned sleep.

"You be careful using that phrase, mister," she warned him leaning over near his chair. "Goodnight...'Daa-Dee'."

Gabrielle's voice was syrupy sweet when she teased him as she walked from the room.

"Hey, hey!" Nathan called sternly, sitting up and frowning. Smoke sat up too. Nathan stroked his fur.

Gabrielle laughed aloud as she ran up the stairs. Nathan chuckled to himself as he eased back down on the recliner.

"Daddy indeed," he mumbled, shaking his head. He smiled, replaying the word over in his mind as he drifted off to sleep. Smoke looked up at his master and just like Nathan had trained him to do; Smoke's paw hit the button on the recliner for the heat massage.

Gabrielle looked around the spacious guestroom. Blue walls, gray woodwork; the room looked regal. She was surprised to see that the bed had a canopy. It was a deep royal blue, the same as the bedspread and curtains. The furniture in the room was marine blue and closer examination told her it had all been made by hand. It was a gorgeous room. Nathan was a talented man. *Yes indeed*, she thought as she flopped across the bed, *my mother would truly adore you, Mr. Nathan.* "Correction," Gabrielle said aloud, "my mother probably adores you already." She drifted off to sleep.

CHAPTER XIII

Jimmy was angry and it was late. He had left Brandeis's house at seven and afterwards he managed to get away from the Durango. *Who was that anyway?* Since he had never seen that SUV before, Jimmy did not have a clue. He drove around for a while. His anger was mixed with frustration. He had no idea where Gabrielle was but he was sure Anderson was somehow in the middle of the whole situation. He did not know what he wanted to do but he knew he wanted to get even...with somebody. He stopped at a bar and had a few drinks but even that did not make him feel better. In fact, he was even more agitated after having shoved a few shots of Scotch down his throat. The liquid burned and so did his anger. He steered his BMW toward City Line Avenue. He was determined to let Anderson know that he did not like losing his woman. He would get her back but first, he would make Anderson sorry they had ever crossed paths.

He watched the building from his car for a long time. He had parked across the street so no one would pay real close attention to him. After about twenty minutes, Jimmy had figured out what he was going to do. He waited until someone was exiting the building. One of the women from the housekeeping staff was leaving, so he hurried past her mumbling something about forgetting his keys.

All of the offices like the accounting firms, the law offices and investment companies, in the Parkline Building on City Line required special security because of the valuable, confidential paperwork they maintained or the special nature of the work they did. Rayzor-Sharpe Security and Private Investigations, Inc. was no exception. None of that mattered to Jimmy. He was a man on his own mission. Once inside the building, he checked out the lobby. He walked over to the security station. The surveillance cameras and the computer were on. The security guard could be seen in one of the hallways. He appeared to be making sure certain offices were locked. Jimmy laughed to himself. While security is much tighter during the day, these places tend to be more relaxed at night. Jimmy went to the elevator. He did not have to wait long and once inside the elevator, he pressed the button for the fifth floor. He looked out into the lobby one more time to make sure the guard had not returned. The elevator doors closed.

By the time Jimmy reached the fifth floor he was smiling. He had already decided that an electrical fire would be the more effective way to destroy all the records in Anderson's company. It would do considerable damage to the equipment and furniture too. More than anything, Jimmy wanted to strike out at Anderson for making him look bad, for taking Gabrielle, for being his half-brother, for being successful and for anything else that came to his mind. Jimmy was doing a slow burn inside and suddenly, he wanted Anderson to burn too.

Jimmy swayed a little bit while standing in front of the office door. The alcohol in his system was really beginning to effect his balance.

"They're supposed to be such fancy big shots; driving around in that big lim-o-zine," he said out loud as he steadied himself. "I bet they didn't even change the locking system." Jimmy snickered as he pressed the buttons on the keypad to unlock the office door. The first time he tried, he missed the pad twice as he pressed in the four-digit code he had used during his first break-in. He had trouble pressing the "Enter" key. He rocked on his heels for a minute before trying again.

"Humph!" he mumbled, "I must have had more to drink that I thought."

He staggered a little but finally steadied himself long enough to press the "Enter" key. What happened next caused Jimmy to almost sober up. An alarm went off! It was nothing like he had ever heard before. At first, he was frozen in place. Then, when he saw a light go on in the inner office, he realized someone would be at the door soon. Jimmy ran to the end of the hall and quickly down a flight a stairs to the fourth floor. He stumbled a bit but managed to open the door and ran inside. He pressed for the elevator. When he looked at the panel and noticed an elevator coming up, he figured it might be the security guard. He took the stairway to the third floor and forced the fire escape exit door. Fortunately, it opened and he was able to leave the building. He ran down the fire escape to the alley at the rear of the building. He did not notice anyone chasing him yet and was able to make it to his car and pull off. He almost had an accident. He drove into a hospital parking lot off City Line Avenue and waited until his heart rate slowed down. "Oh man, that was too close!" His stomach suddenly burned and his head hurt. Jimmy opened the car door and gave up his lunch.

"So, they **are a little** smarter than I thought," Jimmy sneered after he got himself together. "They changed the locks after all. Okay fine! But that only slowed me down. It won't keep me out. I'll be back!" He remembered the movie where he had heard that line and he laughed loudly. "Yeah, baby, I'll - be - back!"

Anderson had fallen asleep in his office. After he had taken Gabrielle to Nathan's house in Willow Grove and helped her get settled, he had returned to the office to do some work for a few of his clients.

He had given a report to Mr. Duvall concerning his stolen artwork. He had traced the art to a dealer who had noticed it at an art show and saw it again later, when some "questionable characters" tried to sell the pieces to him. They fled when the dealer asked too many questions. Anderson decided to use his street contact. He would report back to Mr. Duvall in a week.

Anderson had also spoken to Mrs. Montgomery. Missing persons were his best and worst cases. He loved it when he was able to reunite long lost family members. He hated it when he had to be the bearer of bad news. He told the woman that her daughter had been found but she was critically ill in a hospital in Pittsburgh. She needed a blood transfusion. Mrs. Montgomery would have to hurry if she wanted to see and possibly even help her daughter.

That phone call had caused him to think about his own situation. He had started the search for his mother while he was on the police force but he had not devoted a lot of time to it. He had high hopes that after all this time his mother had also been searching for him. Her task would have been easier because except for the traveling he did during some of his cases; Anderson stayed pretty close to home. If she had wanted to find him she would not have had a problem. Anderson, on the other hand, had run into one stumbling block after another. During her modeling career, Cassandra had altered her appearance often. Sometimes, she even changed her "stage" name in order to advance her popularity in the media.

Although legal records Anderson had searched revealed that she had never married, his mother had attached "Mrs." to her name on several occasions. This usually happened whenever she was photographed with some VIP. If it appeared in the society section of the paper, other reporters would call her for an interview. CaSandra would somehow let it slip out that they had secretly married. Once she had milked the publicity for all it was worth, she'd let slip that they had secretly divorced unless the alleged spouse vehemently denied the marriage had ever happened. Then, she would go into hiding, claiming to be overwrought.

Anderson had stretched out on the couch. *Just for thirty minutes*, he thought, but he had fallen into a deep sleep. He had been asleep for almost two hours when the alarm sounded and startled him. He realized how tired he was when it took him a few minutes more than usual to get his bearings. As soon as he remembered where he was, he bolted from the couch with his revolver in hand. He sprinted to the door; de-activated the alarm and went into the hallway just in time to see the door to the stairway closing. He ran down the stairs but he lost the person he was chasing on the fourth floor landing. As soon as he heard footsteps, he went down to the third floor and saw a man leave through the door of the fire escape. Instead of following him, Anderson ran to a window in the third floor hallway. He watched from the window facing the street and saw a young man running. He observed the familiar black BMW as it emerged from the shadow of trees and sped away.

"Jimmy!" Anderson said the name as if it were a bad word. He turned away from the window and took the stairs back to his office. A security supervisor was waiting by his door. Anderson put his gun back in his shoulder holster. As he stepped toward him, Anderson noticed that the security officer was frowning.

"We saw someone run across the street, Mr. Ray. My partner chased him but the guy got in a car and drove off." The guard shook his head. "The way he was driving, it's a wonder he didn't run into somebody."

"Don't worry about it, Hank," Anderson replied. "I know who it was and I can almost guess what he intended to do."

"Do you want to file a report, Mr. Ray?" the young guard asked.

"No, not this time," Anderson said shaking his head and patting the young man on the back. "There was no real harm done. Besides, I know exactly where we can find our little 'weasely' friend if necessary." The guard nodded and walked toward the elevator.

Anderson checked the outer office door again. It wasn't damaged. He went back inside to get his things. He turned off the computer and grabbed his jacket and briefcase. He turned out the lights, re-coded the security lock and left the building. Once in his car, he dialed Nathan on his cell phone.

"Talk to me," Nathan answered on the first ring.

"Our friend has been busy," Anderson told him.

"Really? What's **his** problem?" Nathan sat up. Smoke sat up and looked at his master. Nathan stroked the cat's neck and Smoke settled back down.

"I suppose it's get even time," Anderson answered, "at least, that's what I think he came to do, all things considered."

"You mean Gabrielle's moving?" Nathan asked.

"Among other things," Anderson responded.

Nathan immediately knew that Anderson was referring to the fact that he and Jimmy were half-brothers. If Anderson knew, Jimmy had probably found out by now too.

"I'm not sure what he intended to do but there was a latent liquor smell in the hall."

"Ah-ha, drunk and stupid! Well, that just means he'll be back and probably sober next time." After a slight pause, Nathan added, "Want me to go by the office?"

"No, Nate. There was no major harm done. He didn't have time but I do agree with you. No doubt, he'll be back."

"Yeah, mama probably taught him never to leave a task unfinished," Nathan replied absently.

"What? Where did **that** come from?" Anderson asked.

"Forget it!" Nathan responded sharply shaking his head. "I'm just tired," he added.

Anderson frowned. He had never known his godfather to make an analysis without a reason.

"You okay?" Nathan asked after moments of silence passed.

"Yeah," Anderson answered, "but I had to call Mrs. Montgomery. This one was hard, Nate. Her daughter could die. I didn't tell her that but the doctor will. There's nothing else anyone can do."

"Look Air," Nathan spoke carefully to his godson and friend, "you know how it is in this business. Sometimes, no matter what we do, the news is bad and nothing, 'cept maybe God can change that…but we keep doing what we do because people need us. That's why we started and that's why we keep going." There was silence on the other end of the phone.

"Sometimes the outcome can be everything we don't want, but Air, you **did find** the woman's daughter. Hopefully her mother will get to her in time." Nathan waited to make sure

Anderson was listening. He heard his friend let out a deep breath.

"Look at it this way," Nathan continued, "if not for this line of work, you might not have met Gabrielle. The results of this situation are good and I might add, getting better by the day. She found the courage to leave that little weasel. All we did was provide the means to the end."

"Yeah," Anderson said finally, "I guess you're right. How is she doing?"

"Probably sleeping by now. It's been a long day. I'm gonna turn in too. You, my man, should do the same."

"Yes, Da-Dee," Anderson replied sarcastically in a falsetto voice.

"Hey, chill! I've already been called that **once** today."

"No kidding? By who?" Anderson asked curiously.

"Gabrielle and I were talking about her mother."

Anderson started to laugh. "Say no more," Anderson told him, "I can just imagine what happened. Talk to you tomorrow, Nate." Anderson hung up, still laughing.

After Nathan hung up the phone, he set the cat on the floor. He got up from his chair and turned off the light in the room. "Bedtime Smoke," he told the cat as he turned on his alarm system. He also set the motion detectors for the outside grounds. After what Anderson told him, Nathan did not trust Jimmy. He was pretty certain the young man did not know where he lived but he also knew Jimmy was resourceful.

Smoke was already halfway up the stairs when Nathan followed. Nathan glanced at Gabrielle's closed bedroom door. The area under the door was dark. Nathan smiled, hoping she was sleeping peacefully. He went to his room down the hall.

Nathan's room was green. Walnut-brown paneling covered two walls halfway up and there were several art pieces on shelves on the painted portions. He had a plush beige carpet on the floor. A bright orange tiger seemed to leap from the brown Oriental rug on the wall at the head of his bed. In the middle of the room was Nathan's big, round bed. The one luxury he

101

promised himself when he was on his own. Nathan wanted a large bed that would always accommodate him no matter how he slept in it. The round bed was perfect. He changed into his tan pajamas and turned out the light. He opened his dark green drapes and let in the moonlight. Then Nathan climbed into bed. After a few minutes he sat up.

"Smoke, why did you let me do that?" Nathan said as if chastising the cat. Smoke looked up from the other end of the bed. Nathan got out of bed and knelt down to say his prayers. Something he'd done all his life since age three.

"Merciful God, it's me again. I've been blessed with so much, I have to say, 'thank you.' I come to You one more time because You already know my dilemma. You know how difficult the last ten years have been. I've loved Air like a son; the son I never had. Yet, I've had to keep things from him and it has been nothing but torture. I know that once everything is out in the open, I could lose my godson and God, that would just kill me inside. I had hoped no one would ever get hurt but since I've concealed some hard truths for so long, there's no way it won't be painful. Now, it's just a matter of time. I really don't know what to do except to keep telling You how sorry I am. I pray that someday, he'll be half as forgiving and just as understanding as You are. Anyway, thank you for watching over him and allowing me to be part of his life. Thank You for all the blessings You've given me, especially lately. Amen." Then he climbed back into bed.

Jimmy had gone back to the apartment. It was late. Eleven o'clock. He tried to watch television but Gabrielle's absence was getting to him. He went to the refrigerator and got a bottle of beer. He drank half and angrily put the bottle down. He flipped off the TV and grabbed his jacket. He swore as he stood up.

"If you think I'm gonna spend the night alone just because you ain't here..." Jimmy said out loud, "well, that ain't happenin'.

Jimmy picked up the phone and dialed a number.

"Yo Shirley," Jimmy barked into the receiver, "What do you mean 'who's this,' you didn't say that last week. Yeah, that's right. It's Jimmy. I'm on my way over. Yeah, it's late, so what. I **said**, I'm on my way...Naw, she ain't here. Why you askin' 'bout her anyway? That don't have nothin' to do with you an' me...That's why I'm callin' to let you know I'll be there shortly. Yeah, Baby. I'll buy you breakfast in the morning. Sure, sure, whatever. Right, Baby, see you soon."

Jimmy hung up and walked out the door. He looked up in his rearview mirror as he climbed in his BMW. "Who da man?" he asked as he looked up. "Nobody but you, dude, he said answering himself. "Oh man, I'm trippin'," he laughed and started the car.

CHAPTER XIV

Sunday morning, Anderson's phone jarred his sleep at six a.m. He learned over and hit the speaker button. "This better be good," he replied, annoyance in his voice.

"Yo man, you think I like makin' calls this early?" a raspy voice asked on the other end of the line.

"Skeeter! So why **did** you crawl out of your hole so early?"

"Hey man, is your machine broke? I tried calling you yesterday."

"I turned it off, Skee. Sometimes I need some rest too," Anderson informed him.

"I can dig it. The superheroes took the day off. Hey, why not, since you got the rest of us..."

"Get to it, Skeeter! Why are you calling?" Anderson barked.

"Okay, okay, don't get hype. You told me to let you know if I heard anything about the artwork. Now you know, that ain't really my thang but there's been some noise," the informant told him.

"What kind of noise, Skeeter? For the kind of money you charge me, this better be good," Anderson warned.

"You'll get your money's worth. Ma facts is **all-ways** valid," retorted Skeeter. "Anyway, does the name Salvadore DelPontee mean anything?"

"Yeah, half a dozen things and **all bad**," Anderson answered sitting up to listen better.

"Well you can add art to the half dozen," Skeeter replied smugly.

"I'm listening," Anderson said sharply.

"I hope so, this **ain't** my time of day. Anyway, there's a rumor that two large vans will be pulling into Fairmount Park near Thirty-third and Columbia next Friday night. Actually, more like Saturday morning 'bout three or four in the a.m. Seems this guy, DelPontee will be pickin' up a few items, if you know what I mean."

"Yeah, come on, Skeeter, talk to me." Anderson urged.

"Some of the stuff is s'posed to be items lifted from the two art shows in New York and DC," Skeeter continued.

"How do you know it's what I'm looking for?" quizzed Anderson.

"Would I be callin' this time of day if it wasn't? We, vampires like to sleep."

"Okay, Skeeter, get to the point," ordered Anderson.

"**Point is**…" Skeeter retorted, "these guys who stole the art grabbed some pieces that belonged to that local rich guy. His stuff was on loan to the New York Gallery. It got ripped off. These dudes tried to fence it but nobody's buyin'. The rich guy is makin' too much of a stink; you know…offering rewards and all? So, none of the regulars will touch it. These turkeys thought they'd try to ransom it back but that didn't happen!"

"Next thing I'm hearing; they contacted DelPontee. For some strange reason he's into buyin' art, this week anyway."

"How do you know all that, Skeeter?" Anderson probed.

"Boy!" said Skeeter, "a Brothah's gotta work hard for some cash! Hey man, you know me. I keeps my ear to the ground."

"Careful Skeeter, you could wind up with a very dirty ear," Anderson cut in sarcastically.

"Very funny. **This**—is the thanks I get when all 'm tryin' to do is help a Brothah out? You know what 'm sayin'?"

"Yeah right, Skee. Then, why is your help so-o-o expensive?" Anderson asked.

"I gotta eat, yo. It ain't easy out here, okay? But…if you don't want my help jus'…"

"Chill Skeeter!" Anderson ordered. "You'll get your money; same time, same place as always."

"Yeah Air, it's cool. Oh and tell Nate, that's his name, right? Tell him to bring a hearty meal this time. I'm a growing boy." Skeeter laughed out loud.

"**Boy?**" Anderson frowned as he picked up the receiver. "You're almost **thirty-two!**"

"Hey man, quiet. My boyish looks and charm keep me alive out here. I still pass for twenty-five when I can. Anyway, don't forget what I said, okay? I'm out." Skeeter hung up.

Anderson sat on the side of his bed going over all the information Skeeter had supplied. Anderson had been taking notes on his pad. He looked at the paper and frowned. This bit of information would cost him three hundred dollars. Still, it was the best lead he had gotten in weeks. Skeeter could be a pain but his facts were as he put it "all-ways val-id." Skeeter had been very helpful to Anderson on numerous occasions in the past.

Anderson had been investigating a sting operation when he and Skeeter first met. The young man was running a con on a known extortionist. Anderson kept Skeeter from being the victim of revenge in exchange for information.

After their first run-in, Anderson had Skeeter checked out. He found out that Skeeter was no dummy except for the fact that even though he had graduated in the top ten of his class with a Bachelor's Degree in Business Administration, he chose street life to earning honest wages. Skeeter made his living conning con artists. He called it getting even. He once told Anderson that "doin' the 'stablishment thang" bored him to death. Anderson had known Skeeter for almost three years and was becoming more concerned about his informant and friend. He really liked Skeeter and certainly did not want to read about him in a tragic news article. Nathan had once suggested that they hire Skeeter on "non-establishment" terms but make his situation more legit than it is now. Anderson was now re-considering his original refusal. "After all," Nate had reasoned, "Skeeter could probably go places neither of them could."

Anderson smiled as he lay back down. Finally, he had a possible break through on the one case that had taken a lot of his time and attention. Anderson could not help thinking about his very, lucrative client.

Mr. Jason Duvall, one of Philadelphia's rich philanthropists. He was well known as the African-American king of community service. In and out of foster homes as a child, he learned the real estate business and after some incredible closings, success became his middle name. He was constantly in the news for all of the community work he did. Anderson remembered reading how, after the March, Mr. Duval rounded up a group of ex-offenders and they re-habbed a whole city block. Then, he helped each one of them find employment. As far as Anderson knew, they were still working except one.

Anderson was certain Mr. Duvall would be pleased when his artwork was recovered. He had already paid Anderson a fifteen hundred-dollar retainer to recover his stolen possessions. Anderson recalled his first meeting with the balding, middle-aged man. Mr. Duvall had photos of all his art pieces except one, his most recent acquisition.

"I don't care what you have to pay," he'd told Anderson intently, "you **must** get back my portrait of 'The Lonely Woman'."

"The Lonely Woman," Anderson said out loud, bringing his thoughts back to the present. He sat up and swung his legs over the side of the bed. "Where have I heard that before?"

Suddenly his alarm clock sounded and he realized he had to get ready to meet Nathan and Gabrielle for church.

Gabrielle was waiting on pins and needles in Nathan's living room on Sunday. Anderson was picking her up for church. She had not seen or talked to him at all yesterday. It seems as if everybody decided to sleep in because of the heavy rainfall on Saturday. The only thing Gabrielle did was talk to her mom on the telephone. Later, she unpacked her bags and put her things away. She did finally tell her mother that she was staying at Nathan's house. She told her how fatherly he had been toward her. Brandeis told Gabrielle that she was relieved that her daughter was safe.

Gabrielle could not help but tease her mother about Nathan and Brandeis gave up the details of the day she met him. She confided in Gabrielle how much she really wanted to be more than a friend to this man.

"I'm glad you've found someone nice, Ma-Dear," Gabrielle had told her.

"He is so-o special. I know I've only seen him a few times but Gigi, when you get to be my age there are some things you just sense about people. Gigi, Nathan's everything that your dad…" Brandeis's voice trailed off. "Oh Baby, I'm so sorry. I promised myself that no matter how things were, I would never speak ill of your father."

"Mom, it's okay, really," Gabrielle said in a reassuring voice, "I know my dad was no angel but I don't hate him. I just don't know him anymore. He was somebody I barely knew and he abused you. I don't even think about him anymore."

Their conversation shifted into a lot of girl talk about men in general. Then, it shifted again to Nathan and Anderson with mother and daughter comparing notes and laughing. The two ended their conversation exchanging "I love yous" and looking forward to Sunday morning.

As Gabrielle sat waiting for Anderson, her talk with her mother drifted in and out of her thoughts. Every time she thought of Anderson or her mother and Nathan, she smiled. Thoughts of Jimmy put a frown on her face. She was certain she was not going to let him back into her life. She was starting fresh after a good night's sleep. It seemed only right to begin by going to church with her mother and her new friends.

Friends; that is exactly how she thought of Anderson and Nathan in such a short time. Nathan had been extremely nice yesterday. He showed her around his place and helped her to get familiar with her surroundings. He'd made sure she had everything she needed. He explained his security system and told her what public transportation was near his street.

Later in the evening, over dinner, Gabrielle told Nathan that she would be going apartment hunting in a few days. Nathan assured her that even though he understood her anxiousness, she did not have to rush.

"It's more important that you're safe," Nathan had told her thoughtfully. "When we can be sure that Jimmy is no longer a threat, that will be time enough to look for your own spot. Besides, I have more than enough room."

Gabrielle had learned a lot at dinnertime. First, she discovered that Nathan loved to cook. As they sat eating lamb chops, mashed potatoes with gravy and turnip greens, Gabrielle wondered why some woman had not snatched this man a long time ago. She decided that she had not known him long enough to ask but she was quite pleased that he was growing fond of her mother.

Nathan was an animated storyteller too. Gabrielle went from giggling to full-bodied laughter several times during his stories of his godson's antics as a young boy. His favorite story was about the time Anderson fixed him and his grandfather pancakes for Father's Day. Anderson was only nine years old. He begged his godfather to come over for breakfast because he was cooking! Gabrielle almost fell off her chair in hysterics as Nathan described how he and Anderson's grandfather struggled to eat the three-inch thick pancakes while Anderson watched proudly. "It took me two weeks to jog off all those pounds!" He'd confessed while she laughed. Nathan swore her to secrecy, telling her that Anderson would probably hang him upside-down if she repeated any of what he had told her.

Gabrielle developed a new respect for their friendship as she listened to this man talk about his best friend's son. She observed that Nathan spoke of Anderson more like a son than a "nephew" or a godson and she knew that Anderson's feelings ran just as deep. She was proud to know them both.

While she was waiting for him to arrive, Gabrielle thought about the first time she saw Anderson. So tall and handsome and that voice! She wriggled her toes and put her stocking feet into her shoes when she heard the doorbell. Gabrielle stood up and checked her black and gold pleated skirt before walking to the door. Smoke, who had been watching her from his bed near the fireplace, went with her.

Anderson was opening the door as she reached for the doorknob. He had been rushing to be on time so he was a little out of breath. Anderson turned the key in the lock and the doorknob in one effort. He was moving so fast; he had to steady himself at the sight of her. He straightened to his full height, looked at her from head to toe and smiled.

"I didn't think it was possible," he told her as he stepped into the hallway.

"Hey Smoke." He greeted the cat that was circling his feet and then turned his attention back to Gabrielle.

"You didn't think **what** was possible?"

"For you to look twice as pretty as the last time I saw you," he answered.

She blushed as he handed her a single long-stemmed rose. She looked at the rose and ran her finger along the stem. "It's **de**-thorned," she looked at him with pleasant surprise.

"With **these** two hands," he stated, holding them up in front of him." The florist offered but I wanted to do it myself."

"It's a sign of caring to de-thorn a rose," she stated softly.

"I know." Anderson's voice was heavy with emotion.

Their gazes locked and something intense, yet unspoken passed between them. Anderson cleared his throat, breaking the silence. "Shall we go?" he asked reaching for her hand.

"Just a minute," she said as she eased away from him. She ran and got her gold jacket and black pocketbook from the sofa. Anderson helped her put her jacket on and she glanced down at the cat.

"See ya later, Smoke," Gabrielle smiled at him adding, "that is, **if** you're still here when I get back, you ol' player."

"So Nate told you about his 'lady-killer' cat, huh?" Anderson mused. Gabrielle nodded.

Smoke stopped grooming himself long enough to look up at her. Gabrielle blew him a kiss and Smoke tilted his head to the side as if to receive it.

"Hey, get your own woman," Anderson said looking down at the cat frowning.

Gabrielle laughed and Smoke resumed his grooming.

Anderson re-set Nathan's security system as they walked out of the house. He escorted her to a silver gray car and she came to a halt. She was looking at an unfamiliar Cadillac. Anderson grinned as a curious frown crossed her face.

"Don't worry, it's mine," he told her and laughed as her eyes widened.

He helped her into the car. Once he got into the driver's seat he watched her as she sniffed the rose. A smile eased across her face.

"Now, **that's** what I like to see," Anderson winked at her. Then he started the car.

Anderson asked Gabrielle to read the directions that Nathan had written down and left with her. Anderson slowed down as they neared Brandeis's church and his eyes widened in amazement. He wondered how he could have lived and worked in the city so long and not have noticed this completely circular, dome-shaped structure before today.

"I don't believe it," he finally said out loud. "It's round! The church building is completely round."

"Well, not quite," Gabrielle replied. "There's an education center connected to the rear of the building and it's rectangular. There are two tunnel-like hallways that connect the buildings. We can go from one building to the other without having to come outside. We, women are very grateful for that on rainy days." She playfully patted her hair and smiled. He chuckled. After pulling his Cadillac into the parking lot, Anderson helped Gabrielle from his car. He had not let go of her hand when they walked slowly toward the front door.

CHAPTER XV

Second Chronicles Christian Fellowship Center, besides it's unusual name, was a sight to behold. It was the first church Anderson had ever seen with a solar structure. The building stood one and a half stories high and it's grounds covered four-square city blocks. Anderson noticed that the entrance was wheelchair accessible. Instead of steps, the front of the edifice had a very wide ramp with a railing. There were narrow stained glass windows with a three-color pattern of orange, yellow and blue. A different color in the shape of an angel alternated in each window. There was a banner over the front door that read, "Enter to be Blessed. Exit, to be a Blessing."

"Did you know that from the sky people say that this building looks almost like a musical note?" Gabrielle said.

"Really? Who was the architect that designed the church?" Anderson asked as they walked up the ramp. He held the door for her and several other women who were going into the church.

"Pastor's father. He's an engineer and licensed contractor. He said something about keeping a promise to his son once he went into the ministry. He had help from a very special member too, Mr. Jason Duvall. They..." Gabrielle did not get to finish.

Anderson stopped so abruptly Gabrielle almost tripped since he was still holding her hand. Anderson steadied her.

"Sorry," Anderson replied when he realized that he was the reason she lost her balance.

"What's the matter?" she asked when she saw the strange look on his face.

"Did you say 'Jason Duvall'?" He asked as he raised a questioning eyebrow.

"Yes. He's one of our more faithful members. Why?"

"He's a client of mine," Anderson informed her. "You said 'our'; so, this is **your** church too?" he asked.

"Mama wouldn't have it any other way. While living with Jimmy, I wasn't coming that often because he didn't like it. But that's no longer going to be a problem.

"Ya got **that** right!" Anderson almost snarled. He made a face of disgust at the mention of Jimmy's name. Gabrielle squeezed his arm as if to reassure him as she spoke again.

"Air," she spoke quietly for only him to hear, "please, don't worry, the decision I made earlier is final. Jimmy is part of yesterday. I'm moving on now. Case closed."

He touched the hand on his arm and smiled at her. He looked around and saw people watching them. Many of the women looked at him and then smiled at Gabrielle. Anderson was puzzled.

"Quite a few of the members who'd seen him, didn't like Jimmy either," Gabrielle told him. Anderson nodded his understanding. He noticed some of the women still observing them.

"We'd better go inside." He gestured toward the double doors to the sanctuary. He paused. "Gabrielle, could you do me a favor? If you see Jason Duvall this morning, show me where he's sitting. It's important." She nodded as they started toward the middle doors.

"Oh, that'll be easy," she replied, frowning toward the ceiling. "Let's see, third pew…middle aisle, right hand side of the church."

"All the time?"

"For the last five years," Gabrielle smiled and added, "he likes Mama."

Again Anderson stopped short but this time Gabrielle did not trip. She did frown again.

"Sorry," he said sheepishly. "You mean Nate has competition?"

"No, not really," Gabrielle responded taking Anderson's hand again. "Mama once said she can't stand balding, middle-age men."

"But Nate is…" Anderson looked at her confused.

113

"**Nathan**," she said emphasizing his name, "is the exception. Trust me. Besides, he's bald by choice, not circumstance. Anyway, something happened to Mr. Duvall last year. It seems like he has another interest but no one knows who she is."

Just then they spotted Nathan walking toward them. They looked at him and then at each other and smiled.

"**Definitely** the exception!" they said in unison, then had to cover their mouths to keep from laughing out loud.

Nathan had been watching the two of them from across the lobby when they had entered the building. Hand in hand and smiling. They were so into each other, it was as if no one else was around. He decided to give them those few moments before greeting them. It made him feel good to see his godson happy. Gabrielle seemed to do that for him. As he walked toward them, he noticed an exchange between them that puzzled him. When they smiled at him, he returned their pleasantries but could not help but wonder what the topic of their conversation had been. He had a feeling he knew but he dismissed it without saying anything.

"Hey you two. Come on. Service is about to start."

As they walked to the double center doors, Anderson noticed three plaques over the doors. The Scripture from Second Chronicles Chapter 7, verses 11 through 15 were inscribed on them. It touched him. Remembering the pledge they took that day at the March and reading it again, brought back such memories. Gabrielle squeezed his hand as they went through the sanctuary doors.

Nathan led them down the center aisle to the fifth pew on the left-hand side of the church. Brandeis moved toward the middle of the pew as they joined her. Gabrielle sat next to her mother, Anderson was next to Gabrielle and Nathan sat on the end of the row. Once they had greeted Brandeis, Anderson looked across the aisle and sure enough, Jason Duvall was in the third pew. Mr. Duvall had looked over and frowned when Brandeis moved away from the aisle seat. When he saw Anderson, he quickly turned away.

The service started with the processional of the choir. They came in singing "Glory, Glory Hallelujah" and it was not long before Anderson and Nathan joined the singing with the church members. Brandeis and Gabrielle looked at them in surprise and they began singing too. Anderson and Nathan were enjoying the service right along with everyone else.

Jason Duvall was sitting exactly where Gabrielle said he would be. He looked toward Brandeis and his expression changed to disappointment when she did not stay seated at the end of the pew. He noticed Gabrielle next to her. He knew she was Brandeis's daughter. When he spotted Anderson, he raised his eyebrows in surprise and quickly took his attention back to the front of the church. He glanced back again and his eyes caught Nathan's.

Suddenly, Jason Duvall's face took on an expression of sheer fear. He looked as if he had seen a ghost. He turned away abruptly and pulled out his handkerchief and wiped his brow. For a few minutes, Nathan glared at the back of his head. Then, he too brought his focus back to the church service.

Anderson noticed when Nathan stiffened in the pew. He turned to see his godfather's jaw tighten. He looked across the aisle to see Jason Duvall turn around for the second time and then he witnessed the panic that crossed the man's face. When Mr. Duvall looked away, Anderson saw that Nathan continued to stare at the back of his head. It was not the look of a jealous man. It was the look of an angry man, a very angry man. Then, just as quickly as it came, the hard expression was gone.

Midway through the service, after the announcements had been read, the pastor stood up and went to the pulpit. It was time to welcome the visitors but he signaled for Mrs. Johnson, the church secretary to take her seat.

Rev. Lonnie Evans was rather young to be a pastor. He was only thirty-three. Gradually, while Lonnie was still in high school, he had been groomed to handle a few of the church responsibilities. Lonnie's father had chosen a different path for his life. He helped his son with different projects but he had never felt the call to the ministry. By the time his grandfather, the church founder had become ill, Lonnie had already assumed some of his grandfather's duties. Since he had several associate ministers to help him, "Rev. Lonnie" quickly became the "acting" pastor of a congregation of two hundred people. When his grandfather died and at the urging of his father, the congregation voted and within one year after being licensed and ordained, Lonnie Evans became the Under Shepherd of the church. Two years later, he attended the Million Man Mach with his father. After that experience, things changed rapidly within the church. The membership grew to three hundred and fifty in the next year. The most impressive part of that information was that one hundred of those members were under eighteen. At the same time, by a unanimous vote, the church's name was changed from the Sixty-sixth Street Fellowship Church to Second Chronicles Christian Fellowship Center. Lonnie's grandfather was still recognized as the founder.

As the congregation gave him their undivided attention, it became clear to any visitor that the members loved, respected and even protected their young pastor.

Attendance was high this morning and the membership was quick to get settled in their seats.

"Good morning, Brothers and Sisters," his voice was enthusiastic as he addressed his members.

"Good morning, Pastor."

"You all…well, most of you know me well enough to be aware of how I might sometimes change the order of service in midstream," he said slowly.

"As the Spirit leads," the congregation responded. "Praise God," he said just as slowly.

"And I try," he replied a little jokingly, "**not** to be too long-winded," he said smiling.

The members laughed at the understatement.

"But believe me when I tell you that I have to make a change this morning. My eyes have seen a sight that brings joy to my soul." He smiled again.

"Some of you know my testimony. I told it after I returned from being a knucklehead. Yes, I was a knucklehead. I was on a path to destruction."

Some of the older women nodded in recognition.

"I was eighteen," he continued, "and I wanted to be as far away from here as I could get. I was failing in school...giving my mom and dad a hard time and I stopped coming to church." He turned to look at his father who was sitting in the front pew to his right.

"To this day, I believe some of my behavior was what made my mother physically ill."

Some of the elder women groaned. Some said "My Lord" and he continued.

"My mother grieved over me. Young people, we sometimes cause our parents to do that." He waited for his words to take effect.

"But sometimes there is Someone bigger in the plan of life and no matter what we set out to do, we **can** be interrupted."

Some of the deacons said "Amen" and Rev. Evans focused his gaze in a specific direction.

"Sometimes Almighty God will send someone to interrupt us. It happened to me and Brothers and Sisters, it might happen to you one day. The day you choose a wrong direction." There were more "Amen's" from the congregation.

"There I was eighteen years old, barely going to school and failing everything. **But** because my life was not supposed to be a failure, I was rescued from myself by someone...picture this...three years **younger** than me." He made a face. "Sorry folks, I don't have time for an English lesson right now." Some people laughed while others nodded in understanding.

The church was quiet. Everyone was so still it was not hard for Gabrielle to notice when Anderson suddenly shifted in his seat. For some reason he looked very uncomfortable. Gabrielle tilted her head to see Nathan. He had a slight smile on his face. She turned her attention back to the minister.

"I want you to know that I did not make it easy for the young man who volunteered to tutor me. I was arrogant and defensive. He was fifteen and in the tenth grade because he'd been pushed ahead. I was eighteen in the tenth grade because I'd been foolish several times. While others were advancing, I was being...left behind. And it was my own fault."

This time, Brandeis looked around. The entire congregation seemed to be captured by the story this charismatic man was telling. Brandeis looked beyond her daughter. Anderson seemed uneasy. She thought he was enjoying the service. She looked to the front again.

"This young man knew I resented him but he was a very astute individual. He realized that I must have wanted to finish school. I was still there even though I was failing. I could have dropped out at any time. And here's something else, he didn't hold his age or mine, over me. He came at me where I live." He had their attention now, so Rev. Evans explained.

"We met at a playground. I was playing basketball. I always did when I was avoiding home or homework. My soon-to-be tutor challenged me to a game. After he beat me, twice; we made a deal - as long as he could beat me, I had to cooperate and let him help me with my schoolwork. But the first time I could beat him at basketball, he would stop tutoring and leave me alone. In the end, we **both** graduated with honors." Rev. Evans smiled with pride.

The congregation applauded. There were cheers. Some said "Amen."

"Some would say...that this means I'm lousy at basketball," Rev. Evans injected when the members grew quiet. The congregation laughed and some of the men teased him. He took it with a good heart.

"That will be our next fundraiser over at our community center. Who can go one on one with the pastor?"

The members laughed again. Rev. Evans smiled and then his face grew serious.

"God has answered my prayer, Brothers and Sisters," he said slowly. He looked up at the ceiling and blinked hard, clearly holding back tears. "That man, to whom I am so grateful, is here today and although I've prayerfully said 'thank you' many times, I was not able to properly say it to him. Until today. Brothers and Sisters, I'd like you to meet my very good friend and my high school tutor, Anderson Ray."

The congregation was applauding. Anderson had closed his eyes and was shaking his head with a no-he-didn't-just-do-that expression. Gabrielle and Brandeis were looking at him with their eyes wide in amazement.

Anderson stood up slowly and reluctantly made his way to the front of the church. Rev. Evans made his way down the steps from the pulpit. The minister was a bit shorter than Anderson so when he tried to put his arm around Anderson's shoulder everyone laughed. The two men also laughed and exchanged a brotherly hug.

"See ladies, there are **still some** good men out there," the minister said. "Although, it would seem that this one might be taken," he added as he turned his attention to Gabrielle.

She immediately dropped her eyes and tried not to blush as Brandeis let out a loud, "Amen!" The whole church laughed at her enthusiasm. Gabrielle looked at her mother and made a face and Rev. Evans and Anderson chuckled. Nathan just sat quietly grinning.

"Air," the Reverend began when the humor subsided..."that's what we called him in 'da hood'," he told his people. "Air," he began again, his voice full of emotion, "I want to thank you properly; here and now, in front of all these people. Especially the young people. If it wasn't for you, I might not have finished high school and I know I would not have gone to college and...I probably would never have been around to do this—." He raised his hands and extended them toward the membership.

"I thank God for you, my friend and I hope I made you proud." Rev. Evans's voice broke as the two men hugged again. Mr. Evans, Sr. rose from his seat and gave Anderson a hug and a pat on the back. He took his seat again and he too, was misty eyed.

The people were ecstatic. Many were applauding. Some were praising and some were crying. Anderson turned away from the people trying to conceal his tear-stained face.

Rev. Evan's gave him another pat on the back. Anderson turned back to face everyone as the minister spoke again.

"My friend, I want you to know that we try to give the young people here...exactly what you gave me, a chance. Some of them get a second chance but more important; some, get their **first** chance"

The two men shook hands and then Anderson tried to go back to his seat. Rev. Evans was still grasping his hand. "Would you like to say something to everybody?"

Anderson shook his head. He was still very filled with emotion.

"Then would you do me a favor? Could we sing the song you taught me? The one that helped me keep going whenever it got rough?"

Anderson raised his eyebrows questioningly.

"The one we used to sing together," Rev. Evans reminded him. Anderson nodded as he remembered it.

"Is it all right if I ask my godfather to play it for us?" Anderson asked him.

The minister nodded and Anderson motioned for Nathan to come up front. Brandeis and Gabrielle exchanged expressions of wonder. *These two men are full of surprises.* Nathan went to the front of the church, shook hands with Rev. Evans and then walked to the piano. After a short introduction and once Rev. Evans handed Anderson a microphone and took one for himself, the congregation heard an upbeat version of *"Please, Be Patient With Me," originally written by Sim Wilson, Jr. It did not take long for the entire church to rise to its feet, all except for Jason Duvall. Some of the members observed Brandeis and Gabrielle beaming with pride as they too got caught up in the chorus of the song:

*"Please, be patient with me, God is not through with me yet.
Please, be patient with me, God is not through with me yet.
When God gets through with me—When God gets through with me -
I shall come forth; I shall come forth...like pure gold."©1980

The two men sang the duet with a fervor that had everyone clapping and singing with them. All could see how much the words of the song meant to their leader. He sang with tears in his eyes and a divine love in his heart that he extended out to each one of them, not just on Sunday, but all the time. This was a special service. Gabrielle, for one, was glad she came. She would have regretted missing any part of it.

After the song, the two men exchanged another brotherly hug. Nathan hugged each one of them also. Then, he and Anderson returned to their seats and the rest of the service continued as originally planned. When they sat down this time, Nathan sat between Brandeis and Gabrielle. Anderson sat next to Gabrielle and at the end of the pew. He could observe Jason Duvall clearly but chose to pay more attention to the service. He planned to speak to his client after service.

After service, Brandeis, Gabrielle and Nathan went to greet Rev. Evans and his father.

When Anderson saw Jason Duvall standing in a corner of the room alone, he went to speak to him. He greeted a few of the members who came over to say hello and shake his hand. When the small crowd dispersed, Anderson made his way to Jason.

"Mr. Duvall," Anderson greeted him matter-of-factly.

"Good morning, Mr. Ray. Or should I say good afternoon," he replied looking at his watch.

"Good Afternoon, Mr. Duvall. I just wanted you to know that with the new leads I have, I will be able to recover your stolen merchandise." Anderson kept his voice low and was standing very close to Mr. Duvall so their conversation could not be overheard by anyone.

"That's very encouraging, Mr. Ray. I was wondering when all the money I've been paying you would bring some results."

"I earn every penny, Mr. Duvall and I have the expense receipts to prove it," Anderson informed him. "Of course, you know that some of my information sources won't exactly be claiming what I pay them on a tax return."

"Meaning I have to take your word for some of your expenses. No matter, after what I heard here, today; I believe I can trust you." He paused and looked around. Jason leaned closer to Anderson. "You didn't forget about the main item I mentioned did you?"

"No, Mr. Duvall. I'm very close to finding it and I should be getting back to you soon," Anderson assured him.

Jason Duvall nodded. Then he and Anderson shook hands.

"I **need** that painting Mr. Ray, and I'll pay. I don't care who I have to pay, I just want it back," he said emphatically.

"I understand, sir."

Anderson observed his client one last time. He was a professional looking, brown-skinned man of medium height and build but with a profound presence that was hard to ignore. Still, Anderson sensed that there was something else. Ever since he became Anderson's client, Jason Duvall seemed to be a man obsessed.

Brandeis, Gabrielle and Nathan were already outside in the church parking lot when Anderson joined them. They had been laughing and talking. Suddenly, they all stopped. Anderson thought he had walked up on some secret conversation until he realized that they were all looking in the same direction.

"Our pain-in-the-neck is on surveillance," Nathan told him pointing across the street.

As soon as Anderson noticed Jimmy parked across the street from the church, Jimmy pulled off, screeching his tires as he left.

"I say, da boy do know how ta make a exit," Nathan said in his best Foghorn Leghorn voice. Everyone laughed and Brandeis threw her hands on her hips.

"What?" Nathan asked feigning innocence.

"Thank God, a man who loves cartoons as much as me, I mean I...oh, forget it," she said frustrated.

"Don't-cha worry, Mama, yo' English be just fine by me," Nathan said clowning.

"Oow," Brandeis made a face like she had eaten something sour.

As they all laughed, Nathan took Brandeis by the hand and walked toward his van. Anderson and Gabrielle stood watching them.

"Well, good-bye to you too," Gabrielle called sarcastically.

Nathan and Brandeis turned and waved and then continued to walk away.

As Anderson and Gabrielle walked toward his car, they heard a car engine that sounded loud and fast. When Jimmy pulled up this time, his car blocked the exit to the church parking lot. From his vantage point, he could see Anderson and Gabrielle. He stared at them and fumed. He was so consumed with anger; he did not hear the car horns of the drivers who wanted to leave the lot.

Two members, who also acted as church security, went running toward Jimmy's car.

"Sir, you'll have to move your car. People want to leave," one of the guards told him.

"In a minute," Jimmy snapped back as he craned his neck trying to see where Anderson and Gabrielle went.

"Sir, you must move now or we'll have to call the police," the other guard told him.

Jimmy looked at the man, and then he tried to look for Anderson and Gabrielle.

"Where'd they go?" he asked out loud talking to no one in particular. He tried to search for them again only to be confronted by security once more.

"Sir," the first guard said more forcefully, "please move your car, now!"

Jimmy pounded the steering wheel, then shifted his car into drive and sped away. Anderson and Gabrielle had been sitting in his car. Anderson had decided that it would be safer to remain where they were until Jimmy drove away. Once Jimmy pulled off, Anderson started his car. He had driven about six blocks when he realized that Gabrielle was crying.

Anderson pulled out of traffic and parked. He turned to face Gabrielle. When he reached for her hand he realized she was trembling. He took both of her hands in his.

"Hey Gigi, don't let him get to you. We won't let him hurt you," he told her gently.

"**I** won't let him hurt you," he said in a stronger tone.

"Why won't he just leave me alone? It's not like he will be alone. He has Shirley."

"You know about her?" Anderson asked as he reached in the glove compartment.

Gabrielle nodded, "I guess I just didn't want to face it but I knew there was someone. Then, one day, she actually called the house. I saw her name on the caller i-d."

She wiped her eyes with the tissue Anderson provided. "It sounds like you knew about her too," she added.

Anderson let out a slow breath before he spoke. "I just didn't know how to tell you. Nate and I checked Jimmy's background. As smart as he is, he's been doing some pretty stupid things. We dug a little deeper once I discovered he was my half-brother. Nate got the police report and I got the…'street' report. That's when I found out about Shirley. Gigi, I was going to tell you when I thought you were…"

"Air," Gabrielle interrupted, squeezing his hands, "I'm not upset with you. I knew there was something going on with Jimmy. For a while I ignored it. I guess I hadn't decided what to do about her or about them. Once I knew, it hurt so much that I was full of indecision about so many things. But now, I'm not."

Anderson put his arm around her. He was not worried about Jimmy following them because Jimmy had only seen the Pathfinder. Since he did not know about the Cadillac, Anderson was pretty certain they would not be approached.

"You know what I think now? I think I had to make my decisions all at once. I mean making a clean break away from the whole relationship. Otherwise, I probably would not have said anything to him about Shirley. Whenever I complained about anything he would…" Gabrielle's lip started to quiver, and she lowered her head.

Anderson saw the pained expression on her face and did his best to comfort her.

"Gigi, that's over now. He won't ever put his hands on you again. I promise. Nate and I will do whatever we can to make sure that Jimmy understands that you walked away from that kind of treatment for good. I just need to know that you're sure this is what you want."

When Gabrielle raised her head she looked right into his eyes. "I'm not going back, Air. I never want to see him again. Even though I know that they don't always help, I'm filing for a restraining order tomorrow. Jimmy might not honor it but at least he'll know I'm serious."

Anderson used his index finger to wipe a tear from her cheek. "Gigi, he's probably twisted this and thinks I took you away from him. Especially since, I'm sure by now, he knows that I'm his brother."

"Air, the two of you may have the same mother but you are nothing alike. So much for genes."

Anderson smiled at her attempt to lighten the mood.

"My decision to leave Jimmy was just that—mine. Meeting you may have helped a little but I've known for a long time that I had choices to make. All of my mother's warnings did not fall on deaf ears. Something I saw on television the other day made me finally realize that I had to decide my future." Her voice trailed off.

"Nate's sister, Ruby," Anderson said as he re-started the car.

"You saw it too?"

"No, but I know Ruby. She and Nate had been going 'round and 'round about her boyfriend for a long time. He'd talk to me about it sometimes. Neither one of us could understand how she could keep going back to that nut. Their biggest argument was because Adam put her in the hospital."

Anderson gripped the steering wheel and Gabrielle reached over and touched his hand. She saw the tenseness in his jaw and lightly squeezed his hand.

"Ruby realized that it would get worse if she stayed. She finally decided to leave for good. She's doing just fine now and that 'fool' as your mom would say, is in jail."

There was a dull silence in the car before Anderson spoke again.

"Gigi, Jimmy won't ever touch you again," he said firmly.

"Does this mean that I'm now one of your clients?"

"No," Anderson said as he pulled up to Big George's Restaurant. He turned to look at her. "No, Baby, this time it's personal."

He spoke with such finality in his voice that Gabrielle did not comment. Even after he helped her from the car and they entered the restaurant together. Jimmy's name did not come up in conversation again. Instead they spent the afternoon getting to know more about each other and discovering the things they had in common. They talked about their professions, their families and their favorite past times.

After dinner, Anderson took Gabrielle back to Nathan's. They sat and talked over cheese and crackers and tall glasses of iced tea. Gabrielle shared some anecdotes from happenings with the students at school and Anderson talked about some of his funniest cases. They both noticed how easily they talked to each other. When they had been laughing and teasing one another for a while, Gabrielle realized that this was the first time she could talk freely with a man and not have to apologize for what she said. Anderson did not seem to be easily offended or overly sensitive about minor things. Gabrielle had been laughing for a while when her expression changed to serious.

"What's the matter?" Anderson asked when he noticed the change.

Gabrielle smiled. He didn't miss much. "I want to ask you something."

"Then ask. Why would you hesitate?"

"We've just become friends and I don't want to pry into anything that's none of my business," she answered frankly.

"Ask whatever you want. I'll let you know if and when you're being too nosey." He tweaked her nose gently trying to put her at ease.

"OK. Why did you go to the Million Man March?"

Anderson looked surprised by the question but he appreciated her curiosity. There was a long pause before he responded.

"At first, before I decided to go, I guess I was just curious. Nate told me that he was attending some of the planning meetings so I went to one with him. There was so much strategy and planning was extensive: mapping out pick-up sites, handling phone calls and giving final instructions to everyone. I got so caught up in the preparations, it just made sense to go."

"I used to get upset when I thought about all the critics who had something negative to say. Some thought it was a "Muslim" thing and I guess I did too, at first. But I changed my mind about a lot as the date got closer." Anderson closed his eyes when he felt himself getting choked up. He paused to get his thoughts together before he continued.

"There was so much going on that day. Nate, my granddad and I drove to D.C. We saw other cars along the way. Some had signs that let you know where they were going. Some drivers who had room in their cars or vans even picked up Brothers along the way. We even met some men who decided to make the journey on foot. That blew me away!"

"Really?" Gabrielle's eyes widened in amazement.

"Oh yeah. When we stopped, they decided to rest for a while. We ate together and got acquainted. These were some nice guys. Before long, we were kidding around, laughing and acting like family. We had prayer together and went on our way and so did they. They wanted to keep walking so we gave them some sandwiches. When they finally got to Washington, we all applauded and cheered. Gigi, so much went on that day; rich, not so rich and poor standing side by side. So many Christians and other men in one place; I didn't know that many had even decided to go. Oh, there were men there from many denominations, from many different walks of life but Gigi, **we** were surrounded by men who knew the Lord, personally. There were so many prayers lifted up that day. So many prayers for family situations, for jobs, for men who made the decision that day to come back to Christ."

"Another amazing thing was that my granddad stood for all that time and never once complained about being tired. And the Pledge; it still sends chills through me when I remember what we promised God. Some people don't believe it but many lives were changed for the better. My grandfather told me later that he was blessed to see such an awesome sight before he died."

Anderson rested his head on the back of the sofa and blinked his eyes. There was a mellow silence between them until he looked at her again. They did not realize how long they had been talking until Nathan walked in the door.

"Hi Nathan," Gabrielle greeted him first.

"Hey Nate," Anderson said as he stood up.

"Air. Gigi." Nathan was using Gabrielle's nickname for the first time. She blushed and dropped her eyes.

"Hey," Anderson looked from Nathan to Gabrielle. "I'm supposed to be the only one who makes you do that." Anderson pretended to be hurt. Nathan blew a breath on his fingernails and rubbed them on his lapel.

"I got skills," he bragged, teasing his nephew. He grinned broadly and Gabrielle laughed once his dimples appeared. Anderson threw his hands in the air and rolled his eyes toward the ceiling.

As Gabrielle observed the two of them she smiled. She enjoyed their playful exchanges. Watching the two of them, she imagined that this is what it must be like between a father and son with a good relationship. At least, it had to be pretty close to the real thing.

"Your mother said she forgives you," Nathan told Gabrielle as he sat down. Anderson and Gabrielle who were seated on the sofa exchanged questioning glances.

"You told her that you would spend today with her after church," Nathan explained.

"Oh my gosh!" Gabrielle exclaimed as she threw her hand over her mouth. "I forgot."

"She figured as much, considering…" Nathan said as he looked at Anderson who suddenly looked like a sheepish little boy.

"I'm sure you provided a nice distraction," Anderson replied confidently.

"My man, don't cha know that's right!" Nathan countered smugly. He observed the two of them for a moment and smiled to himself. He got out of his chair and looked at them as if he was about to say something. He shrugged and turned to leave.

Anderson looked at Gabrielle. "What was that about? Sometimes, the man's so hard to read," he told Gabrielle. Anderson could tell that Nathan wanted to say something but he appeared to have changed his mind.

"No-o. Not impossible," Nathan replied when he stopped in the doorway, "but Air, I think I just might be..." he looked at Gabrielle and then at Anderson. "never mind," He turned and exited the room.

"Hey Nate, wait up," Anderson said jumping up from the sofa. He stopped Nathan at the stairs and frowned. "If you need to talk about something, I mean, what were you going to say? You think you're what?"

"Sorry Air, I'm not ready to talk about it yet." Nathan's voice was as low and serious as the expression on his face. He saw the concern on his godson's face and added, "maybe later, okay?" Then he quickly went upstairs. His cat, Smoke followed him.

Anderson came back in the living room and stood near Gabrielle. When she looked up at him questioningly, Anderson shrugged. Gabrielle rose from the sofa to face him.

"I wonder what's gotten into him all of a sudden?"

Gabrielle gave him a knowing smile. She touched Anderson's hand lightly. He caught hold before she could pull away.

"What? Gigi, if you think you know, tell me," he implored.

"Not yet," Gabrielle shook her head. "Nathan will, when he's ready. You'll just have to be patient." They looked at each other for a long moment, both of them unsure what to say next.

"Well." Anderson looked at his watch. "I guess, I'd better be going." Slowly, they walked hand in hand toward the door. "Call me tomorrow if you need me."

"I'll be all right. Nathan is going with me. At least I know Jimmy won't be waiting outside of school for me since it's closed for summer vacation. I've even arranged to change my college classes to daytime for the summer. He only knew my schedule for night classes."

She noticed the brief look of disappointment on Anderson's face. She knew it was probably because she was not asking him to go with her. She reached up and boldly touched his cheek.

He shut his eyes against the warmth of her hand. Then he opened them slowly and looked at her. He pressed her hand against his face.

"Air, we both know I need to do this alone. The only reason I'm asking Nathan to go with me is because I agree with both of you. Jimmy is dangerous. But if you go with me and he sees us together; well, it's just like you said, it will just fuel his anger. I need for him to know that it's over but I'm not deliberately trying to rub his nose in the fact that you and I will probably be seeing a lot more of each other." Her voice died down as she ended the statement. Then she blushed.

"So, you do still care about him?"

"Not that way," she reassured him. "I'm just not a vengeful person. As much as he hurt me, hurting him back won't solve anything. Besides...I don't want us to start off like that."

"Us?" Anderson raised an eyebrow hopefully.

"Yes us." She adjusted his necktie with both hands. She brushed some imaginary lint from the jacket of his suit at the shoulder. He caught her hand and kissed it. She looked deep into his eyes.

For the first time, Anderson pulled her to him and hugged her. Neither of them said anything. They just stood embracing for a long moment. Finally, Anderson let out a long, slow breath and Gabrielle pulled back to face him. He rested his forehead against hers.

"One day at a time," he promised, "we'll take it one day at a time."

She nodded. As she stepped away from him, she took hold of his hand. That's when Gabrielle noticed the sterling silver identification bracelet on his wrist. She raised his hand to examine it more closely. The inlaid oval shaped stone set to the left of his name particularly fascinated her. She ran her finger over the smooth surface of the stone.

"What's this?"

"My birthstone."

131

She frowned. She was familiar with all of the birthstones. She'd never seen anything like this before.

"When is your birthday?" She was trying to guess what kind of stone it was. It was so unusual, dark in color but with flecks of red, green and blue within. It was very pretty.

"October," he told her knowing it would not help. He smiled at her. She was trying to be so subtle. The stone was rare. He knew she would never guess. When he saw her frown, he decided her curiosity had suffered enough.

"It's a 'Black' opal, Gigi, they are harder to find than the white ones. It was different and unique, so I wanted it."

"Yes, because that's just like you," she said in a mellow tone, "different and unique." She applied gentle pressure to his hand.

The compliment delighted him but it threw him a bit. He was not sure what to say so he cleared his throat.

"I guess I'd better go. Long day tomorrow," he lied not sure what else he should say to escape an awkward moment.

"Thanks for today, for dinner and everything else." Gabrielle dropped her eyes. She focused on the hand she was still holding.

He raised his hand bringing hers with it. When she looked up at him, he kissed the back of her hand.

"I did no more than what was supposed to be done." He told her. "You deserve to be treated special, Gigi, no other way. Whatever I've done, it was all for you." His voice was low, husky. She felt that tingling in her toes again. He unhooked the I D bracelet and raising her left hand, he fastened it on her wrist. It was a little large for her so he hooked it in one of the links that fit it closer to her wrist.

Her eyes gleamed. "Oh Air, no. I couldn't." She tried to take if off but he stopped her.

"Just for tomorrow," he told her, "since I can't go with you, treat it like I'm still close. Wear it for me. You can give it back when you return from the courthouse. That is, if you still want to give it back."

Gabrielle didn't dare speak. She nodded and gave him a half-hearted smile.

"Call me tomorrow?" He reminded her as he brushed his index finger across the tip of her nose.

"Sure." She smiled again.

She closed the door behind him and leaned her back against it. Smoke came down the stairs and circled her feet. "Oh Smoke," she sighed as she bent down to scratch the cat behind his ears. He purred loudly as she picked him up. "I know just how you feel," she told the big cat smiling. *I could purr too.* "Yes sir, I know just how you feel." She put the cat down and went back into the living room to turn out the lights.

I know how you feel too, Nathan said to himself. He had observed Gabrielle and Anderson at the front door from his vantage point at the top of the stairs. He wasn't spying on them. He had planned to go downstairs for some hot tea but once he realized where they were, he decided to allow them their privacy. He backed out of sight and waited. Neither of them seemed to realize that if Smoke came down the stairs, Nathan was not too far behind him. They were too pre-occupied with their own conversation to pay the cat much attention and at that moment, they were certainly not thinking about its owner.

As Nathan watched Gabrielle, he compared her to his sister. Each had so much love in their hearts, giving it to the wrong kind of man. Each of them had high hopes that the man would change and when that did not happen, both women were faced with some tough choices. Thank God both women made the right choice.

Nathan went back to his room once he realized that Gabrielle would be coming up the stairs soon. He left his door ajar because he knew Smoke would come looking for him. Sure enough, Smoke eased his way into the room but Nathan was surprised when Gabrielle unexpectedly knocked on his door. He looked up from a book he pretended to be reading as he told her to come in.

"Hi Nathan."

"Hey there, how you doin'?" He smiled at her, his deep dimples showing.

Gabrielle's smile widened as she stepped around the door.

"I came to thank you for everything, especially for offering to go with me tomorrow."

"No thanks necessary. It's more of a favor to your mother than to you. I like to know her mind is at ease especially after what Jimmy pulled today," his voice trailed off. Gabrielle nodded.

"Well, see you in the morning, Nathan."

They both said "goodnight" and she closed his door.

CHAPTER XVI

One week later…

Jimmy paced around his mother's apartment like a caged animal.

"For crying out loud, will you sit down!" his mother yelled.

He threw himself on the sofa. "A restraining order!" Jimmy shouted. "She got a Restraining order against me. She got it on Monday. I actually got a subpoena at work and had to go to court yesterday. I can't believe it. I thought we had something going. I ought to…"

"You'll do nothing right now," his mother snapped.

"But Mom, the cop came to my job, to my job, Mom."

"Oh stop whining. It's not like you've got a good job that you'd lose. You take off anytime you want anyway. I don't know why Sal puts up with you," his mother scolded.

"Cause, I'm your adorable son, what else," Jimmy sniped sarcastically, "besides," he continued before she could respond, "I'm good at what I do and he knows it. Without me to ferret out his information he would not be able to do all that insider trading or keep track of all his gambling."

"Keep your voice down," CaSandra warned. She stumped out a cigarette as she got out of her seat and walked to the window.

"Aw mom, give me a break. Nobody's here but us. You act like the walls got ears. If they did, he'd have been caught a long time ago with all the college football and basketball games he's fixed and the other illegal gambling. Let's face it, Daddy Dearest has got it going on." Jimmy walked over to the wall unit and turned on the stereo. His favorite FM-station was on so he turned the volume up.

"Satisfied?" he snapped at his mother. He started dancing to the music.

CaSandra stood by the window watching her son. That fool could move. She remembered that he never had any trouble getting girlfriends in high school. She wasn't real crazy about his "love 'em and leave 'em" attitude but she understood it. Of course she understood it, she had spoiled him. Jimmy was good-looking and he knew it. CaSandra knew it too. She did make some pretty babies. CaSandra's thoughts wandered to Anderson and she made a face. She had seen him once or twice since he had grown up. Yes, she had made two pretty babies.

Jimmy saw his mother watching him and used the opportunity to show off. Even as a young boy, he'd learned every dance as soon as it came out. Dancing was something Jimmy could do with ease and he loved being the center of attention. He had even taught himself some tap dancing steps and later, convinced his mother to pay for lessons. He always entered dance contests being careful to pick just the right partner. As a teenager, he practiced often with his mother who was also a good dancer. She helped him mix steps from old and new dances together. He tried anything that would get him noticed. That was how he met Gabrielle.

She had attended one of those theme parties with some friends. He came because his friends told him about the thousand-dollar cash prize. The party had a disco theme and Jimmy was dressed in the obvious white suit with black silk shirt. Gabrielle's friends had jokingly said something about the "Dance Fever" wanna-be until the dancing started. Then, they were all trying to get to dance with him.

The night they met, Gabrielle had ignored him. Jimmy hated being ignored. He had asked her to dance three times before the contest and she politely said "no thank you." It quite naturally surprised everyone when he picked the girl in the royal blue rayon dress as his partner for the dance contest. This time, Gabrielle said "yes." Everyone was watching poetry in motion but for Jimmy and Gabrielle it was competition—pure and simple.

Jimmy was amazed. She followed his every move. They were better than any dance couple seen in a long time. When they won the dance contest, they split the money but Gabrielle let him keep the trophy. She had a feeling it was important to him. Right then, Jimmy was hooked. He wanted Gabrielle as much as he wanted the trophy. And so, he set out to have her.

A few persistent phone calls later, they started dating. Jimmy became possessive immediately. He complained if she spoke to any of her male friends when they were out. He yelled at her if she did not pay him enough attention.

"You're my woman," Jimmy would tell her over and over. "Do you understand me?" You are MY woman."

In the middle of dancing in front of his mother, Jimmy's expression darkened. He thought about Gabrielle. They were so happy until...

"We were doing just fine. If he hadn't shown up with his big, fancy ride we'd still be fine." Jimmy said finally.

"You were not," his mother clipped. "I told you dark-skinned people are trouble but did you listen to me?"

"Oh so you can talk. What about big brother?" Jimmy yelled.

"Half brother," CaSandra retorted.

"So what? He's dark-skinned. I don't hear you complaining about him," he reminded her.

"You leave him out of this. We were talking about that dizzy girlfriend of yours. She's nothin' but a..."

"Mom!" Jimmy hollered, cutting her off. "Don't even go there," he warned pointing his finger at her.

CaSandra shook her head in disbelief. That her son would even use a threatening tone toward her was so unreal. When her expression turned to hurt, Jimmy softened.

"Mom, why are you defending him?" Jimmy referred to Anderson with disdain in his voice.

"I'm not defending him. I'm not." There was a long pause before she spoke again with sadness, "it's just that sometimes I wish...I wish I had not given him away. I see what he's done with his life and I know I wouldn't have to be hiding out like this. I could be livin' better."

"Feeling guilty, Mom? Jimmy looked at his mother with a nasty grin. "Having regrets 'cause you gave him away and kept me?"

"Stop it! There's at least nine years between the two of you. My life had changed a lot by the time you were born. I just meant that he's so successful now. I might have been..."

"Living large instead of with a failure?" Jimmy taunted.

"I didn't say that!" his mother snapped.

"But you were hinting at it again. You always do." Jimmy countered, "You're always fantasizing about how it 'might have been.' I just didn't know who you were talking about until now. Well, I'm sick of hearin' it! Nobody told you to get so carried away in the good life that you got hooked on drugs. You did that to yourself. My mom, the high-class model became the high priced call girl and then turned into the low-class..." his voice broke. He did not finish. No matter how much he hated what she did to herself, to both of them, he couldn't hurt her. He loved her. He sat down, raking his fingers through his hair.

"Jimmy, Jimmy," CaSandra replied soothingly, "I know I did you wrong for a while when you were little. There were times I was so strung out I couldn't take care of you. I know you didn't understand what was happening. I'm just glad one of my friends came to help me when you were a baby. If he hadn't stepped in, I know D.H.S. would have taken you away from me. You were such a tiny baby, born premature and all. I know you needed me. Anyway, I was only messed up for three years." She paused and then continued. "But I'm clean today. I've never abandoned you since then have I? I'm here for you now. Once I got straight, I made sure I've always been here when you needed me. I owe you that. I love you, Baby. You know I love you."

She was sitting on the arm of the sofa cradling Jimmy's head against her chest. Jimmy heard the quiver in her voice. He hoped she wasn't going to cry. He hated when she cried because of him.

"Don't you worry, now," she said kissing the top of his head, "we'll make her sorry she left you. I'll make her come back if that's what you want. You'll see"

They sat quietly for a few moments. Mother and son holding each other, locking out the world.

"Mom," Jimmy called her name as if from far away, "You said someone took care of me when you were, you know, messed up? How come I don't remember nobody? Who was it, Mom?"

CaSandra jumped up from the sofa as if it burned her.

"Don't you worry about that!" she scolded. "You just be glad your dad, I mean Sal found us when he did. I should never have tried to run away from him. Honestly, I don't understand these women who run away from men who take good care of them. I mean, so what if he hits me sometimes. He only does it if I make him angry. I shouldn't make him angry. Women do that sometimes; make men angry. Sal is good to me. I mean, look where I am. I live in Center City. Everything I want is right here and just look at all this; nice place, nice clothes," she spreads her arms to encompass the room. "And he gave you a good job. You're makin' nice money huh? Right?"

"Yeah, Mom, my pockets are way deep." Jimmy replied flatly.

"That's right! We got it real good here. We don't wanna mess that up. Do we, Jimmy?" CaSandra grabbed her cigarette pack. She lit one as she walked toward the window. *She's always looking out that window.*

"Mom, all I ever wanted was for you to be happy. Sometimes when I look at you I don't believe you're happy. Maybe Gabby was right to leave me," Jimmy said somberly.

"You hush up! Happy? Of course, I'm happy! Who wouldn't be happy livin' like this?" CaSandra folded her arms across her chest and looked out the window as she took a long drag on the cigarette in her other hand.

"As for you, nobody walks out on my baby. She'll be sorry she did."

She let out the smoke in a long angry blow and Jimmy knew that that meant there was no more discussion.

"You can get her back." CaSandra said finally.

"What are you talking about? Nobody even knows where she is right now." Jimmy told her as he got up from the sofa. He walked over and stood behind his mother. They were the same height so when she turned, she looked him straight in the eye.

"Tomorrow night, Baby," she told him touching his cheek. "If you really want her back, I'll tell Sal. He'll set it up. You'll see."

"Mom," Jimmy said softly, "I don't want her hurt. I just want…"

"I know," CaSandra replied putting her finger to his lips to silence him. "I know." She faced the window again. Jimmy turned and made his way to the door.

"Jimmy," his mother called to him without turning around.

"Yeah?" he stopped but he did not turn around either.

"I love you. You do know that don't you?"

"Yeah Mom, I know." He walked to the door and left the apartment without a backward glance.

Once Jimmy was gone, CaSandra did something she promised herself no one would ever see her do. She stretched out on the sofa and cried long and hard.

When Jimmy left his mother, he decided to take a long drive. He did not have a destination in mind. He just needed to clear his head. His conversation with his mother had been too intense and he felt heavy. Something was wrong and he never liked it when his mom got like this. He always had to give her a few days to change her mood. He started his car and took the quickest route to the Expressway. Then he just drove hard and fast.

CaSandra had dozed off and she woke up to the telephone ringing. She wiped her eyes as she grabbed the receiver.

"Hello? Oh hi, Sal, yeah, I was taking a nap. I had a headache. Yeah, it's gone now. Tonight? Okay, sure Sal, I can be ready by nine. Oh Sal, I have a favor to ask, Sweetie. No, I'll explain when I see you tonight. Yeah…me too. Bye." She hung up and went into the bedroom to get ready to go out.

Her phone rang again and she picked up the red one near the bed.

"Hello?"

"Hey Mama, what's shakin'?"

"Skeeter!" You know you're not supposed to call me. I always call you. I told you this is…"

"Too dangerous. Yeah, yeah, yeah. Sistah, you watch too much TV," he told her.

"Maybe, but Skeeter, if anyone ever figured out that we're…"

"Who's gonna know? I sure ain't tellin'. Last thing I want to do is have a run in with your old man. I don't need that kind of drama."

"Did you give him the information I gave you?" CaSandra's voice was anxious and her eyes kept watching her door.

"Just like you told it to me, Sugah" Skeeter informed her.

"Does he suspect anything? I mean does he know where you got your facts?" she asked.

"Hey! I ain't got 'stupid' tattooed 'cross my forehead, okay? I did exactly what you told me. Besides, what you pay me is far more attractive than what I get from him."

"Are you sure you're okay? I mean, do you need any money?" she asked, trying to change the subject and get him off the phone.

"Three C-notes from him and five from you?" Skeeter laughed. "No Baby, I'm just fine in the cash department at the moment. It's my **other** department that needs fixin'…know what 'm sayin'?" He muttered slyly.

"Skeeter, Honey, I can't. I told you I'll have to call you in a few days after this weekend mess. When things die down maybe we can talk then."

"Don't play me, Woman. You and I've been at this way too long. Tomorrow night all hell will break loose and there's no tellin' where you'll be after that." Skeeter's voice was intense.

She sighed out loud. "All right, Skee. You're right. Meet me at the same hotel we went to last week. I'll be there first thing in the morning. I promise. Sal doesn't stay overnight anymore, so I can call a cab right after he's gone. We're going out tonight but…"

"You're not gonna…I mean, the two of you don't…" he stopped. He could not bring himself to ask the question.

"Aw Skee, Ba-a-by," CaSandra replied in the coyish voice she'd perfected long ago. "Sal and I don't do that. He only has me around for decoration, you know, someone to hang on his arm and make him look good. There's been no one but you for three years now. You and me, Baby. Just you and me. "You **do** believe me, don't you, Honey?" Her voice was pleading but Skeeter knew her well enough to know it could be artificial. Still, she sounded so convincing.

"Yeah, I believe you," he answered. "See you in the morning, Babe."

"See you. Oh, and Skee, I can't wait."

Skeeter made no reply so Cassandra started to hang up.

"Hey Babe?" Skeeter called out.

"What?" CaSandra's voice was anxious. Now, she was going to be late and she still had to get dressed.

"Why are you doing this? I mean, why are you giving Air all this information? You know, if Sal goes down, you go down too. You could get burnt real bad. I mean, you might…and you still won't have your son. He still won't know who you are"

She took a deep breath. Skeeter gripped the phone tighter. He had come to learn a lot about the woman who spent so much intimate time with him. At first, for him it was ego. The whole older woman - younger man thing. But as they spent more time together she began to confide in him. She told him all about Anderson. She knew they were friends. She started paying Skeeter to tell her how he was doing but after a year, Skeeter stopped taking so much of her money. She'd gotten under his skin and now, he was involved for the long haul.

In the beginning, CaSandra had treated him like a convenient past time but he had to believe that over time she really cared. He heard her sob and wished he was there to hold her.

"I owe him, Skee. I owe him the years I wasn't there, the love I didn't give. I owe him so much. This case is his biggest. If I can help him solve it, well, then maybe I will have paid a big part of the debt."

"But Cassi, you could go to jail. You could get hurt. Why don't you let me handle it from here on out? That way, you won't be in the middle and he still won't know that you were the one who had me send the pictures and had me call him with all the leads. I gotta tell you from what I hear, things are getting pretty heated."

"Skee, I gotta go," CaSandra said cutting him off. She hung up quickly and ran into the bathroom just as a key turned in her lock.

Two of Salvadore DelPontee's men entered the apartment and flanked each side of the door. They were big guys who could have easily been part of the Pittsburgh Steelers front line. Their two-piece suits looked uncomfortable but Mr. DelPontee insisted that they be well dressed and "look legit." After their boss stepped though the doorway, the two bodyguards backed into the hall, closing the door behind them.

Salvadore DelPontee was not a bad looking middle-aged white man. Although he was average height, five-seven like Jimmy and average build, he had an air about him that sent a message. The message was "I don't play so don't play with me." Most people got the message with the first look he sent them. Then, in case they needed help understanding; his bodyguards came in handy.

CaSandra was very familiar with that message. Her on-again-off-again relationship with DelPontee had lasted for Jimmy's whole lifetime. DelPontee had taken her by force before Jimmy was born. The one thing he ever regretted doing. He got angry every time he thought about how he lost it over a woman. She made him just that crazy and she wasn't even his...he shook off the thought. He tried not to think "color" when he thought about their situation. These days he didn't even call it a relationship. Besides, he never forced her again. After the first time, she seemed more than willing. He assuaged his guilt by taking care of her and buying her expensive gifts; a car, an apartment, fancy clothes, jewelry, anything she wanted. She accepted it all without hesitation. She was even more affectionate after the gifts. He knew she didn't love him but this was as close as he would probably get. Anyway, he did have something from her that no one else gave him—a son. Jimmy had his brown, wavy hair except his was darker than Jimmy's. They both had green eyes except his were greenish-blue. Jimmy was smart too. DelPontee liked to think his genes had something to do with that. Was that a racist thought? He shrugged it off.

DelPontee's eyes wandered around CaSandra's apartment. He was looking for something, anything unusual or out of place, anything that belonged to a man. He suspected that she was cheating again. She had not invited him to spend the night for a long time. He could force her but he promised himself that would never happen again. He was a powerful man. If all he wanted was to "do it" he could get it anywhere.

It upset him to know that she had "an outside interest." The last time he caught her in her lies; he took his belt to her. And why not? His father had done the same thing to his mother. Made her backside black and blue but she learned. "Sandi" learned too. Until now.

Once again, he suspected she had someone else. It made him mad that he never found out who it was three years ago. Here, she was doing it again; making him look like a fool. If he caught her this time, he was not sure what he would do. His thoughts were interrupted when CaSandra floated into the room.

"Hey Sal, hi Baby," CaSandra cooed as she entered the room wearing a pink silk Versache pants set. She slid onto his lap and applied kisses all over his face and hugged him.

"You're late, Sandi," he barked and swatted her backside, even though he was having a hard time staying angry. She was manipulating him and he knew it.

"I know I'm late and I'm sorry, Daddy honest. I know you don't like it when you have to wait. I'm sorry...I'm sorry...I'm really, really sorry." She repeated the apology between kisses, placing the last one on his mouth. When she felt his lip quiver she deepened the kiss until she heard him moan. She felt him pull away abruptly.

"Stop that," he ordered. I know what you're doing."

"What?" She wore her doe-eyed innocence well. "I'm just glad to see you, that's all and I'm very glad you're taking me out. I've been cooped up in this place so long I was getting cabin fever." She stood up and offered him her hand.

After Sal stood, she linked her arm through his as they started toward the door. CaSandra stopped just before they reached it. She pulled his arm around her waist as she turned to face him.

"Sal, Honey, I want to ask a favor." She ran her fingers up and down the lapels of his navy blue pinstripe jacket. She looked at him through long lashes and knew he wouldn't refuse her anything.

"Sal, this is about Jimmy and that girl," she continued, "now, I know you know how I feel about her, but she left him and Jimmy wants her back. I told Jimmy that you could fix this. I know you can take care of it and it would mean a lot to me, Sal Honey. Do it for our boy, please. Handle it for me, okay Daddy?"

DelPontee ran his fingers through his wavy hair. He looked at the woman facing him.

Oh man, she makes me crazy! Inwardly, he swore to himself. He controlled CEO's, Politicians and Lawyers. He even had a judge or two in his pocket but when it came to this woman, he was weak and he hated it. He knew he would do what she asked. She was his Achilles heel and they were stuck with each other. He nodded as they exited the apartment. At the elevator, DelPontee leaned to whisper something to one of the bodyguards. The big man made no comment. He simply left them and went off to do as ordered. As the two of them entered the elevator with the second bodyguard, CaSandra took DelPontee's arm, her smile laced with malevolence.

CHAPTER XVII

When Gabrielle woke up Friday morning, the house was quiet—too quiet. There was something else; Smoke was sleeping at the foot of her bed. Gabrielle got up and put on her robe.

"Smoke?" she called as the cat sat up, "What are you doing in here, handsome? Where's your master? Where is he, huh? Where's Nathan?"

She walked out into the hallway and didn't hear a sound. Nathan told her that he usually left the house at nine. It was seven thirty in the morning. There was no movement at all except for Gabrielle and Smoke. Gabrielle descended the stairs with the cat on her heels. There was fresh-brewed coffee ready and Smoke had food in his dish but Nathan was nowhere to be found. Smoke went to eat his food and Gabrielle poured herself a cup of coffee.

"Maybe he went to the store," Gabrielle said out loud. She shrugged as she sipped her coffee. She was trying not to associate Nathan's absence this morning to the bits and pieces of conversations she'd heard him having on the telephone last night. He had spoken with Anderson at least three times and each call seemed more intense than the previous one. There were two calls from an unknown source with an unusual name and Nathan even called Brandeis to cancel their date. Although he told her that he could not discuss the case that he and Anderson were working on together; he did do his best to reassure her that he would be careful.

The telephone rang, breaking into her thoughts. Gabrielle waited. Nathan had asked her to let the answering machine intercept the call. She could answer the phone once she recognized the voice. She was glad to hear this one.

"Hey Beautiful," Anderson replied once the beep sounded.

Gabrielle grabbed the receiver. "Good morning." She was doing a poor job of hiding her anxiousness to talk to him but she didn't care. Last night she had been a little disappointed that he had not asked about her when he spoke to Nathan.

"How are you doing?" Anderson asked.

"Just fine and how are you today?" There was a melody in her voice that warmed him. A melody he could get very used to hearing on a regular basis, he told himself.

"I'm okay," he told her as calmly as he could even though his rapid heartbeat contradicted him.

"Air, do you know where Nathan is? It's so early and he doesn't seem to be here."

"Yeah Gigi, I know. We both came to the office early. We have some loose ends to tie up to close an important case. We decided to come in early to do some paperwork. We'll need to get some rest this afternoon in order to go on stakeout tonight."

"Tonight? You mean late tonight?"

"I'm afraid so but don't worry, it will be okay. We'll call for police back-up as soon as we confirm some things." Anderson was trying to convince her that there was no major danger but he sensed that she knew better.

"You will be careful won't you?"

"You think I want anything to keep me from you?"

His words made her feel good. Yet, she was concerned. Nathan's conversation with her mother was so similar to this one, Gabrielle shivered.

"You still there?" he asked when she made no comment.

"Huh, oh yeah, I'm here. Did you say something?"

"Never mind," he said matter-of-factly. He felt a little let down that she might not have heard what he said. "What are your plans for the day?"

"I thought I'd spend a good part of the day with Mom. I need to get back in her good graces after Sunday."

"I know what you mean," Anderson laughed. His mind raced back remembering how they had spent the day. "I guess I could send her some flowers as a peace offering."

It was Gabrielle's turn to laugh. "Well, if you do, you better send Mama flowers and fruit. If you're gonna send her something, you have to do it right to really make her happy."

"Okay, okay. I get the message," he told her laughing. He was glad the mood lightened before he had to end the call.

"Gigi," he paused after he said her name.

"Yes?"

"Fourth of July will be here in a few weeks, what do you say to us celebrating **your** independence?"

"Well, that sounds good, but no matter what we do, we must go to Mama's for her cookout. I have a feeling it is going to be really special this year," Gabrielle said enthusiastically.

"Oh, no doubt. I'm sure it will too, for a lot of reasons."

She sensed a smile behind his words then there was a long pause.

"Gigi?" His voice was low and heavy with emotion.

"Hmmm?"

"You know when all of this is over..." he couldn't say another word. He wanted to, but they would not come.

"I know," she said softly. "See you soon?"

"Count on it," he told her emphatically. Then they hung up.

Gabrielle called her mother and after some catch-up conversation, she told her she would get to her house by one o'clock. She agreed to take a cab so she could bring her laundry. Even though Nathan told her that she could use his laundry room, she declined. She liked the idea of hanging her clothes out in the sun and she was certainly not going to do that in Nathan's backyard. She also knew that if she had to wait for her clothes to dry, she could concentrate on spending time with her mother. On top of everything else, she was trying not to worry about Anderson and Nathan. She knew something about this case was not quite right and she preferred not to think about it too much. Gabrielle sensed danger. Not because of anything Anderson had said. It was truly more because of what he had not said.

Once Anderson hung up after talking to Gabrielle, he had a hard time getting back to work. So far, any talking they did had skirted around the possibility of a relationship. Anderson intended to give Gabrielle all the time she needed but he was also determined to be a very, very good friend. He knew she would be cautious now. A man had hurt her. He had to show her that this man would not.

"That intense look on your face has nothing to do with this case," Nathan said breaking into the younger man's thoughts as he leaned in Anderson's doorway.

Anderson snapped his head up at the sound of Nathan's voice and shook off his embarrassment. "What's up, Nate? I didn't hear you come in."

Nathan frowned. His godson would never have admitted to that in the past. Most of the time, no one was able to sneak up on him. He usually did not let his guard down like that at work. Tonight was a night both of them needed to be very alert. Nathan was concerned but he decided not to mention it. He knew this case meant a lot to the young man. He had every confidence that Air would be fine. Nathan's plan and his long-time promise were to be there as Anderson's back-up, tonight and any other time. Nathan went to his desk and turned on his computer. He made a few phone calls, re-scheduling some of his next week appointments. After this case, he wanted to take some personal time and the beginning of the week seemed as good a time as any.

Anderson rubbed the back of his neck, shook his head and let out a deep breath. Tension. He needed to clear the cobwebs. If he was going to be sharp tonight, he was going to have to focus. He knew something was wrong if Nathan could come that close and he had not noticed. All the training of his profession and his martial arts skills told him that he was off his mark today. He decided that he needed to go home, shower, eat a decent meal and take a nap. As he walked past Nathan, he touched his friend and partner on the shoulder. He mumbled something about meeting him back at the office about ten that night. Then, he was out the door.

While he was alone, Nathan decided to check a few necessary items. His back-up revolver, then Anderson's were loaded. He really did not expect to use them but he believed in being prepared. He placed a call to the local police and Lt. Roberts. He arranged to see him and supply the information about the case, the stakeout and what was going down in the park. Next, he called a friend who always supplied him with electronic equipment. Even though he and Anderson regularly use their cell phones, he wanted two-way radios for tonight. He left the office as soon as he was told he could pick them up.

Nathan was on his way back to the office when he decided to drive by Brandeis's house. In addition to his other errands, he had stopped for lunch and to pick up some dry cleaning so it was well after four in the afternoon when he detoured to Mt. Airy Circle.

As soon as he rounded the corner, he knew something was wrong. He parked quickly and ran up on the porch. The screen door was closed but the front door was wide open. Nathan waited. He listened for movement. He listened for voices. Nothing. He noticed that the wood around the doorway was fragmented. Someone had forced the door open. The black marks around the area suggested the use of a crowbar. Nathan drew his gun and stepped inside.

Nothing was really out of place so there was no sign of a struggle. To Nathan, this meant that there had to be more than one person involved. Even if he had cautioned them against resisting, one person would still have had a fight from these two women. Nathan went into the kitchen, the teakettle was still warm. The break-in was recent. The light in the kitchen was still on. Brandeis's wrap and Gabrielle's jacket were still in the dining room and so were two plates of half-eaten food. This break-in was also sudden. Nathan's jaw tightened as he continued his examination of the scene.

He ran upstairs. The guest bedroom was closest to the staircase and the bathroom was next to it. Both were undisturbed. Nathan grew more anxious by the minute. He cautiously went to the master bedroom and found it in disarray. Several items of clothing were on the bed and the floor. Nathan knew right away that this was Brandeis's room. *Why were her clothes all over the place?* The receiver for the phone was off the cradle. It was lying on the floor as if it had been dropped. Nathan continued to look around. The more he looked, the more worried he became. Thank God he had not seen any blood. *So far.*

Nathan knew he had to call Anderson. *And tell him what?* He wanted to wait until he was sure his hunch was right and he was becoming more certain by the minute. When he was certain he had checked the entire second floor, Nathan went back downstairs. He dialed 9-1-1 from his cell phone and reported a break-in and possible kidnapping. "Victims?" He could only guess how many. One. Possibly two. *And yes, he definitely knew **who** they were.*

When he got to the bottom of the stairs, he sat down. He rested his elbows on his knees, and he cupped his face in his hands trying to think. He took a couple of very deep breaths and stood up. A frown crossed his face. *What was that noise?*

It was faint but he was sure he heard something. He listened again. Just then, he heard the police sirens as they came closer. Be quiet, he wanted to shout. *What **is** that? And where is it coming from?*

The police quickly entered the house and in a matter of minutes they were roaming about, firing questions at Nathan. He had not yet said a word and the sergeant who had been asking the questions began to get impatient, loud and angry. He was about to say something else when Nathan put up his hand, signaling for him to wait. The sergeant stopped everyone except the officers who had gone upstairs. Nathan tilted his head as if listening for something and the sergeant motioned for everyone to remain still. The noise came again. It sounded like something hitting against or rubbing against metal.

"The shed!" Nathan yelled as he ran toward the back door.

Nathan and two police officers were in the yard in seconds. There were several wood planks propped up against an aluminum shed. At first glance, one would think that the shed had been undisturbed for a long time. It was padlocked and with the planks against it, nothing looked suspicious. Yet, the noise sounded as if something was rubbing back and forth against the ribbed door.

An officer returned with some bolt cutters from a squad car and Nathan all but snatched them from the officer's hands. After breaking the lock, he quickly pulled the door open. His heart jumped when he saw Brandeis lying on the shed floor. She squinted as her eyes adjusted to the sudden sunlight and then she shut her eyes as the tears of relief began to come. She was bound with duct tape at the wrists and ankles and lying on her side. Another piece of tape covered her mouth. Nathan lifted her easily and cradled her to him. She rested her head against his chest and let out a muffled sob.

He carried her into the house and placed her on the sofa. The police officers followed. The ones who had been upstairs came down. They were all standing in Brandeis's living room. He ran to the kitchen. A female officer reached for the tape on Brandeis's mouth and Nathan returned in time to stop her from removing the gag.

"Don't!" he yelled, "you'll tear her skin." The officer practically jumped away.

Nathan knelt in front of Brandeis with a basin of water and moistened a towel. He wet the sides of the tape around her mouth and slowly loosened it. When he was sure it would not be too painful, he removed the tape. Brandeis leaned against him. Her hands were still bound behind her so Nathan eased her back on the sofa.

"Easy Brandy Baby," he soothed, "it will be okay now."

"Oh Nathan." She felt her eyes well up with tears that she tried to fight back. She struggled to tell him something but Nathan stopped her.

"Shhh, not yet, Honey. Let me do this first," Nathan said softly.

"Please sir," the woman officer stepped forward. "If she can tell us anything…"

"I said in a minute," Nathan barked back. He pulled a pocketknife from the back of his belt.

"That's not a regulation size knife, sir," the same officer said to Nathan.

"Back off, Rookie," Nathan snapped and in the same minute he cut the tape that was wrapped around Brandeis's ankles. It still clung to her legs so he moistened it, removed it and threw it violently to the floor. He massaged her ankles for a few minutes and heard her moan because of the pain. She had been bound so tightly her ankles had red lines from where the tape cut against her skin. He gently turned her back to him and cut the tape that bound her wrists. Her arms had been secured behind her for so long, Nathan had to help her move them. As soon as she could do so, Brandeis threw her arms around Nathan's neck.

"Oh Nathan," she sobbed, "they took my baby. They took her. They took Gigi." Brandeis held Nathan tight and for a few moments he held her just as tight.

"Brandy Baby," he said as he pulled her arms from around his neck so he could look at her, "WHO took her? When?"

She was crying but she was also angry. She fought for composure so she could explain because the police officers were still waiting to hear what she had to say.

"Two big white men forced their way in here when we came in from the yard. We were out back hanging up laundry and I saw a strange car come around the corner. Something didn't seem right. I'm telling you, Nathan, it was so crazy. The hairs on the back of my neck tingled. I sent Gigi to my room to hide and I decided to try to keep things as normal as possible. When the man knocked on the door asking for Jimmy, I knew something was up. He said he thought Jimmy would be here seeing his girlfriend. That sounded really weird to me so I backed away from the door. When I slammed the vestibule door, I yelled for Gigi to call 9-1-1. That's when the men forced the door and rushed in."

The police officers asked a few other questions and left. Nathan called Anderson who had been taking a nap and let him know what happened. He knew Anderson would come to the house as soon as he hung up. Nathan followed the police to the door assuring them that if he heard anything else, he would call them. Nathan closed the front door as well as he could and went back toward the living room as Brandeis called to him.

"Are they gone?" she asked.

"Yeah they're gone." He gave her a puzzled look.

"Good," She breathed a small sigh as she reached out to him. He went to her immediately.

"Brandy, you're shaking. What's wrong?"

"Nathan, there's something I need to tell you." She tensed even as he was holding her. He moved slightly in order to see her face.

"You said there were two men. Have you ever seen them before?" Nathan asked trying to hide the concern in his voice.

"Not in this neighborhood. Two big, muscle-bound white men. If I had ever seen them before I'd remember. One of them went upstairs and grabbed Gigi…"

"And the other one taped you up?" Nathan asked attempting to finish her sentence.

"NO Nathan, not him; he wasn't the one."

Now, Nathan was confused. "Then, was it the same man who went upstairs? He came down and put you in that shed."

155

"No, Nathan. Please, listen to me," Brandeis's voice broke. She bit her bottom lip as he held her by the shoulders and looked deep into her pleading eyes. Then, her face took on a look of such utter contempt that it suddenly dawned on him what she was going to say before she said it.

"Oh no." was all Nathan could get out before he closed his eyes and shook his head as she confirmed what he feared.

"It was Jimmy, Nathan. Yes, it was. That fool. First, those two men burst in here. One ran upstairs while the other one looked around down here. They only pretended to be looking for Jimmy. When I asked one of them what he wanted, he said this was 'for a friend.' That's when that fool strolled in here! He stood in the hall with this big roll of tape in his hand and a smug grin on his face and then," Brandeis rubbed her wrists where the tape had been too tight, "he just took her."

Nathan took her hands in his. He kissed her wrists and then he held her close to him.

Neither of them saw or heard Anderson when he entered the house. He had heard everything Brandeis said about Jimmy. They did not realize he had been standing there until they heard the screen door slam. Nathan kissed Brandeis on the forehead and told her he would be right back.

Anderson was on the porch. When he stepped out on the porch, Nathan touched Anderson on the shoulder.

"Are you thinking what I'm thinking?" Anderson asked his mentor without turning around.

"That Jimmy is connected to DelPontee somehow? And when we go on stakeout tonight we'll find him, a few answers to this riddle **and** Gabrielle?"

They heard a gasp from the doorway and glanced back just in time to see Brandeis swoon. Nathan caught her before she fell and carried her back to the sofa. Anderson followed him.

"Is she okay?" Anderson asked after Nathan placed a wet cloth on her forehead. Nathan nodded.

"She fainted. I imagine she's exhausted. Air, she was rubbing her feet against that shed door in the yard for over an hour. When I saw her, lying on her side, bound so tight. I just wanted to…" his voice faded as he swallowed the lump in his throat that was mixed with bitter anger.

Anderson was about to speak when Brandeis moaned. Nathan helped her sit up.

"Nathan, Anderson, I'm going with you," Brandeis said intently.

They both shook their heads. "No way, Hon. It's too risky," Nathan warned.

"Please, Nathan, you have to let me go. That fool got the better of me today. He took her and he didn't even let her put her shoes on. Nathan please, I'll beg if I have to but I've got to go with you."

"This is not a competition, Brandy," he told her, using the pet name he had given her recently. "These are dangerous people. Some of them will probably be armed and…"

"And you're not?" She said, patting his shoulder holster through his jacket. "Please Nathan. They took my baby. I let them take my baby."

"Now you hold it right there," Anderson spoke firmly as he knelt in front of her. "None of this was your fault. Two armed men bust in the door, what could you do? It's not your fault and I don't want to hear you talk like that anymore. Promise me," he added, softening his tone while looking at her intently.

Brandeis nodded. "But I still want to go with you tonight. I might be able to help. Her eyes implored as she held Nathan's arm. "Please Nathan, I **have to** do something."

Nathan and Anderson looked at each other. They could talk until they were blue in the face, Brandeis was not going to change her mind.

Anderson stood and backed up. "Your call," he told Nathan as he shrugged his shoulders. Nathan looked up at the ceiling. Brandeis saw his shoulders drop and he breathed hard and wrestled with himself. He understood exactly how she felt. If something happened to Anderson he would feel the same way. When he looked at her again, Nathan gave her a half-smile.

"All right," he conceded, "but you do exactly as I say and **stay** in the car."

Brandeis nodded and dropped her eyes. For the very first time in their relationship Nathan took her face in both hands and kissed her on the lips. She put her arms around his neck as a new rush of tears filled her eyes.

CHAPTER XVIII

Anderson decided to leave his two friends and go to the office. There was no point in going back home so he decided to try to put more information together for the report he would eventually give the police. When he arrived at the office, Anderson felt energized. He was anxious to do something but he knew he had to bide his time. He also knew that Jimmy had taken Gabrielle to shake him up but his brother had only succeeded in making Anderson angry, very angry.

There were still a few hours until the stakeout so he decided to review the information he had in three particular folders: Jimmy's, his mother's and Jason Duvall's.

Jimmy's folder contained a lot of juvenile activity. Break-ins he was suspected of committing; they took place mostly at business offices. In several cases, the charges were dropped. Anderson suspected pay-offs. When Anderson concluded that Salvadore DelPontee was Jimmy's father, he also surmised that many people were "bought off" to keep Jimmy out of jail. Suddenly, Jimmy goes off to school and becomes a decent citizen. Anderson decided that whatever DelPontee was doing now, Jimmy was probably involved up to his neck. He was sure he would be able to prove that later tonight.

Next, he pulled Jason Duvall's file. Rich man, on the threshold of marriage at three different times in his life. So far, everything Anderson found on him depicted a law-abiding citizen. The only piece of the puzzle that did not fit was his obsession with the painting "The Lonely Woman."

Anderson turned on his computer and decided to go on the Internet for more solid information. He explored Art, first and then, Famous Portraits. A more extensive search gave him what he wanted, a photo of the most expensive portrait to be featured in a newspaper article right after it was sold at auction. Anderson printed out the article and enlarged the photo. His breath caught in his throat as he stared at the picture of the beautiful, semi-nude woman partially shrouded in emerald green.

She had posed sitting sideways with her back to the artist but there was no mistaking those green eyes cast in a backward glance over her shoulder. The eyes looking at him from the painting were his mother's!

Something else became very clear to Anderson as he began to piece things together, his mother was also tied to DelPontee somehow. It was DelPontee's men who helped Jimmy snatch Gabrielle and tie up Brandeis and put her in the shed. Obviously, DelPontee was a dangerous man and so were people connected to him. *Was Jason Duvall just an innocent victim? And what was going on between him and Nate?* He closed the second folder.

When he touched the third folder, Anderson hesitated. He had looked at his mother's folder time after time so he doubted that he would find anything new. Yet, Nathan had taught him that sometimes it was good to put something down for a while and re-examine it with fresh eyes later. He scanned the papers quickly, going over her career information and the few facts he had gathered concerning places where she had lived. Next, he went over the personal data he had compiled from telephone calls to other investigators who were also his friends.

As Anderson flipped through the report and other papers in CaSandra's file, he noticed an envelope addressed to him and marked "Personal." It had not been opened. Anderson frowned. *When did this arrive? Why haven't I opened it before now?* There had been so much activity lately, he decided that he must have put it in the folder and forgot about it. Anderson took his letter opener and slit the flap. Inside was a copy of Jimmy's birth certificate confirming the name of his father, Salvadore DelPontee. Also included was a copy of medical records from a local hospital and evaluation reports from a place called Safety Net Drug and Alcohol Rehabilitation Facility located in upstate Pennsylvania.

Anderson expected to see Jimmy listed as the patient who was admitted to the center. He was surprised by his own reaction once he realized that the patient was his mother. He examined the dates of her admittance and discharge.

In the diagnosis and assessment report, Anderson discovered that his mother was in no condition to register herself. She had tested positive for cocaine and alcohol when she was admitted to a local hospital under an alias. She de-toxed there and returned home when she was discharged. No longer concerned about possible negative publicity, in the Fall of the same year, she was admitted to Safety Net using her real name. The mandatory medical examination also revealed that a few months earlier, his mother had had one abortion—illegally. It had been botched so badly that she had to be hospitalized for about a month. She had suffered trauma and depression when she found out that she could no longer have children. She became seriously dependent on the prescription drugs. She was also treated as an outpatient off and on for three years. Anderson squeezed his eyes shut against tears that begged to flow. *Oh Mom*, he thought, *why did you do this to yourself? Dad loved you so much. Why couldn't you just...?* He rested his head against the back of the chair. Those tears that would not be denied ultimately slipped past their barrier. He let out the air that threatened to strangle him and shook his head. He brought his attention back to the document in front of him and looked at the bottom of the second page. Doing some quick math in his head, Anderson realized that Jimmy had to be about three years old when his mother went to Safety Net Rehab Center.

If Jimmy wasn't old enough and my mother was incapable of signing herself into treatment, who did? His eyes caught sight of the name at the bottom of the paper and he frowned. Anderson would recognize this signature anywhere—Nathan Sharpe!

Suddenly his mind filled with multiple questions. *When? How? How long had Nate known where my mother was? Why didn't he tell me? Why wouldn't he tell me?* His head spun as his stomach turned over. One emotion after another collided with his senses: confusion, hurt, surprise, and anger. Anderson didn't understand. He wanted some answers. He wanted them NOW!

Anderson picked up the phone and dialed Brandeis's number. No answer. *Nate probably took her to his place until her door was fixed*, he thought. He called Nathan's house and got the answering machine. Anderson slammed the receiver down.

For the first time, he felt anger directed toward the man who was his godfather, his uncle, his partner, and his friend. He did not like it but it was there and mounting. He decided to try to reach Nathan on his cell phone. As he was reaching for the phone again, it rang.

"Razor-Sharpe," his voice was harsh and he fought hard to hide his disappointment once he knew that the caller was not Nate.

"Yo, yo, you wanna know what I know," the caller said in his usual cavalier tone.

"Oh it's you. What do you want, Skeeter?" Anderson asked in an irritated voice.

"What bug bit you today?" Skeeter's voice grew just as brisk.

"Sorry man," Anderson replied fighting for control, "What's up?"

"Time's have changed and so have the...," Skeeter began but Anderson wasn't listening.

"I don't have time for this now, Skee," Anderson snapped, cutting him off and starting to hang up.

"Yo, hold up," Skeeter shouted in the phone, "I called because I thought you needed to know what I know. The plan for tonight has changed okay? But hey, maybe I should do this later."

"Wait! Whoa. What did you just say?" Anderson's head was clearing.

"Oh, so **now** I got your attention," Skeeter replied sardonically, "I could get killed for even makin' this call an' you busy trippin.'"

"Okay Skeeter, chill. Sorry Man," Anderson stated flatly. "There's a lot happening here."

"You don't say. Well, there's a lot happening **here** too." Skeeter retorted. "In fact, if I don't move my torso soon, I might wind up as part of the happenings."

"Where are you now?" Anderson's voice was anxious.

"Twenty second and Allegheny. Just under the bridge and things are jumpin'," Skeeter told him. "There have been some strange trucks around here all day; all of them have out of town tags."

"So what? You can see a lot of trucks on Allegheny during the day," Anderson said matter-of-factly.

"Yeah, I know, but that's in the mornings. **This** is late afternoon and it is tense 'round here. From what I can tell some of the drivers are strapped, you know what I mean?" Skeeter's voice was on edge and there was a lot of traffic in the background.

"Armed drivers? I don't get it, Skee. But why are you in North Philly?"

"I wanted to check something out before I called you. For some reason this is 'hardware city' and there's been serious money changin' hands."

"Okay, so what's going on and make it fast." Anderson's voice was sharp.

"Cancel the Fairmount Park rendezvous at three a.m. It looks like the delivery will be at eleven tonight down here, near Twenty-second and Westmoreland. That's why everybody's armed."

"What?" Anderson bolted upright in his chair and gripped the phone. "Are you sure?" he asked eagerly.

"As sure as I am that I'm Black and pretty," Skeeter answered. The flippancy was back in his voice.

Anderson got up and looked out the window. It would be night in short order.

"Thanks, Skee, I owe you," Anderson replied sincerely.

"This one's on the house," Skeeter responded. His voice was solemn, mature. It reflected his true age instead of the street-wise kid facade that he usually hid behind.

"Say Air, she's really not so bad, you know?"

Anderson was caught off guard. "What? Who are you talking about?" Anderson was confused.

"Your Mom, she really ain't so bad," Skeeter's voice was soft, in far away thought. Then he was gone.

"What? What did you say, Skeeter?" Anderson shouted into the phone.

It took him a few minutes to realize that Skeeter had hung up.

Anderson did not have time to dwell on Skeeter's last statement or what it meant. He had to telephone Lt. Roberts to apprise him of the changes. The lieutenant was not at the police station so he left a detailed message. Next, he called Nathan's cell phone. When he did not get an answer, he left him an extensive message too. He had just enough time to drive home and change clothes.

Dark clothes were the order of the evening so after a quick shower, he grabbed his black Pelle Pelle baggy jeans and his hooded Handcuffs Sweatshirt. He tied his black Lugz and grabbed his duffel bag containing bulletproof vest and other items essential in stakeout situations.

Anderson was charged. He tried not to drive his Pathfinder too fast down Wissahickon Avenue. His mind raced trying to put the crazy pieces of this puzzle together. He was sure of one thing, tonight a lot of nagging questions would finally be answered. He slowed down as he approached the intersection and parked midway on Twenty-second Street near Westmoreland. He got out of his vehicle when he spotted Nathan's Durango on Westmoreland Street facing the bridge. When Anderson climbed in on the passenger side, Nathan sat up and pushed his cap back from his eyes.

Nathan eyed his godson speculatively. For a second, he thought he saw anger in Anderson's eyes directed at him. He made a personal resolution to get to the bottom of it when this mess was over. He put his hand to his chin and rested his elbow on one of the armrests between them.

Nathan was also dressed in black from his Dickies jumpsuit and black cap to his Karl Kani boots. He was already wearing his bulletproof vest. He was concentrating on the area under the bridge across the street.

A 24-foot moving van was parked on the hill fifteen feet beyond the bridge on the left side of Westmoreland Street. It was facing toward Twenty-Third Street. Its back doors were closed. So far, there had been no movement anywhere near the truck or from anyone inside. Anderson surveyed the area as he was putting on his vest. The streets were quiet and dark but there was undeniable tension in the air. Anderson looked around again.

"Where's Brandeis?" he asked finally breaking the silence as he looked over at Nathan.

"Allegheny Avenue," Nathan said without looking at his godson. "She's in a car parked on the KFC lot."

"You think she's safe there? What if something happens?"

"She's safe enough. She's with Skeeter. He won't let anything happen to her," Nathan told him still looking toward the bridge.

Anderson was uneasy. He wanted to bring up the information he found in his mother's folder. This did not seem like the right time.

"Are there any police here yet?" Anderson had finally noticed that he had not seen any police cars anywhere near the stakeout.

"Not yet but I got a message to the Lieutenant after I got yours from my voicemail."

"You're sure Brandeis is safe?" Anderson asked because he needed something to say.

"Yeah," Nathan responded flatly to hide the concern in his own voice. "Unmarked cars are supposedly on their way and regular squad cars will be in position near the KFC lot and at the gas station soon."

As Nathan spoke, Anderson looked more carefully at the white truck. He noticed a slight movement then nothing.

"Nate, I need to ask you…"

"Shhh, what's that?" Nathan said as he bolted up in his seat.

Anderson turned his attention toward the bridge. A black Town Car rolled slowly down Twenty-second Street. The headlights went off long before the car made a right turn and stopped just under the bridge. The driver flashed its headlights twice. One of the rear doors of the truck opened and a flashlight blinked twice in return.

"Heads up," Nathan said out loud, pulling his gun. Nathan eased out of the van and hid, pressing himself against the wall of the bridge.

Suddenly, from Twenty-Third Street, a black van drove down the hill and stopped almost parallel to the truck and several feet in front of the car. The headlights facing the car revealed the four people inside before the driver of the van, turned them off.

Anderson recognized the driver of the van as soon as he got out. It was Jimmy. He went to the passenger side of the van and opened the door. He took out a briefcase and left the passenger door open.

"Typical," Anderson muttered to himself as he watched.

When two of DelPontee's men got out of the Town Car, Jimmy walked toward the truck. The men stood facing the truck with their guns drawn. Jimmy handed the briefcase up to one of the two armed men standing at the back doors of the truck. DelPontee and CaSandra got out of the back seat of the Town Car and waited.

Skeeter who was parked on the KFC lot was getting anxious. He had been sitting with his window rolled down listening for any unusual sounds. He swore under his breath and reached in the glove compartment. He pulled out the two-way radio Nathan had given him and his .357. Listening on the two-way all he heard was a lot of running. It would start and stop often. Skeeter figured that Nathan and Anderson were moving as close to the action as they could get.

Anderson felt his mouth go dry as he got a glimpse of his mother across the street. He eased out of the Durango and carefully made his way to the opposite side of the street from Nathan. He ran toward the corner and crouched next to a parked car. He adjusted his two-way radio on his shoulder so he could hear Nathan clearly.

Nathan maneuvered his way around the corner and when he was sure he was out of sight he ran across the street. He pressed his back against the projecting wall of the bridge. Very carefully, he began to inch his way toward DelPontee and CaSandra. He stayed close to the pillars of the bridge. Anderson ran across the street making sure the stone wall of the train station concealed him.

One of DelPontee's bodyguards had climbed in the truck to examine the artwork and whatever else his boss was purchasing. Jimmy had stepped back from the door of the truck and was standing near the second bodyguard. Now, he too, pulled a gun from inside his jacket.

Since all attention was on the truck, Gabrielle was able to slide from the passenger seat of the van. It was a little difficult since her hands were secured but Jimmy had made the mistake of taping them in front of her. Since she was shoeless, she managed to drop to the ground unheard and slide under the van. Underneath the vehicle, she remained still until she was sure no one would see her ease to the driver's side and wait for her chance to escape.

"I don't like this," Skeeter said out loud not really talking to Brandeis. "Cassie is going to get hurt." Since she had no idea who he was talking about Brandeis made no comment. Skeeter looked over at Brandeis. He saw a mother in pain. He knew that look. His mother had it on her face often when he was in his teens. He had been a young, foolish kid. Remembering that his mother had taken him to church frequently when he was little, he considered himself blessed that his antics hadn't gotten him killed. Now, he was dedicated to being a kind of Robin Hood in the ghetto. "I'm like Robin **of** da Hood," he would say with that easy-going smile. This is what he would sometimes tell Anderson when he supplied his investigator-friend with information that often put drug dealers and gang bangers behind bars.

Skeeter touched Brandeis's hand lightly. He noticed that she continued to clutch the bag that contained Gabrielle's shoes. He knew she was worried about her daughter. They had talked for a short time after Nathan put her in the car. He couldn't say anything comforting. He was not sure he would have believed it himself. Besides, he was too busy trying to mask his own concerns. He handed her the two-way radio as he opened the door.

"Stay here," he ordered. Then, before Brandeis could say anything, he was out of the car. He remained close to the train station's wall inching in and out wherever the wall jutted. As he stealthily made his way toward Westmoreland Street, he saw Nathan. He was about to cross the street when two shots rang out. Skeeter ducked behind a car.

Suddenly, the other rear door on the truck opened and DelPontee's dead bodyguard was pushed to the ground. The men in the back of the truck started shooting. Another bodyguard was wounded as everyone on the ground ran for cover.

"It's a double-cross! C'mon," Nathan shouted into the radio on his shoulder.

Anderson ran toward the Town Car. Nathan carefully inched his way up Westmoreland Street staying close to the fence of the scrap metal warehouse. He hid behind a pillar of the bridge near a fence.

CaSandra spotted Gabrielle when she rolled to the pavement from under the van.

"Oh no you don't," CaSandra yelled when she saw Gabrielle get to her feet.

When Gabrielle started running, she went after her. Anderson noticed his mother heading up the hill. She was so close and she was slipping away from him again.

Gabrielle didn't see anyone. Once she got her chance, she took off running as fast as she could. It was not long before the balls of her feet hurt each time they hit the sidewalk. Her hands were still taped but she didn't care; she had to get away.

When the shooting started, people were running everywhere. The men on the truck were shooting. DelPontee and his men were shooting. As police arrived on the scene, they were shooting. Bullets were flyin and casings were dropping. Jimmy was taking aim from near the rear of the van. When the ruckus began, he had moved behind the open door of his van for cover. He spied his mother and started to run after her.

"Mom?" he yelled when he saw her going up the hill. She pointed toward Gabrielle and kept running.

Nathan made his way to the front of the truck before anyone noticed him. He recognized CaSandra across the street.

"Cassi!" He yelled and ran into the street toward her.
CaSandra stopped. She knew that voice anywhere.

With all the commotion going on, no one even noticed the driver of the truck or realized that he was still alive. When the shooting started, he had crouched down in his seat. When he saw Nathan run in front of the truck to cross the street, the driver sat up. CaSandra saw the driver. She squinted as she noticed something silver. She had been around DelPontee long enough to know what it was. She ran into the street toward Nathan as the driver moved to the passenger window of the truck.

"NO!" she screamed and threw herself in front of Nathan as the man fired. Nathan felt CaSandra collapse against him as they both fell to the ground.

"You idiot! You shot my mom," Jimmy shouted as he came up on the passenger side of the truck. He fired through the truck's window. The man fell out of sight a minute later.

Jimmy turned the gun on Anderson when he noticed him running after Gabrielle. The heat of his rage rang in his ears. He was about to pull the trigger.

"Don't!" He heard a man's harsh voice behind him. Skeeter was aiming his gun at the back of Jimmy's head. "I'd hate to ruin a family reunion but I will if you don't drop it," he said firmly.

Jimmy placed his gun on the ground and Skeeter walked closer and kicked it away. Jimmy and Skeeter approached CaSandra who lay cradled in Nathan's arms. Skeeter swore. Jimmy fell to his knees in front of his mother.

Gabrielle had stopped short when she heard CaSandra scream and the gunshot afterwards. When Anderson caught up to her, she was leaning against a wall crying. He removed the tape from her hands and she leaned against him. He looked down at her feet; they were red. He didn't even ask her if they hurt. He gathered her up in his arms and carried her back down the hill.

Finally, all the shooting stopped. One bodyguard was dead and so was the driver of the truck. The two men from the rear of the truck were wounded along with the second bodyguard. The police had taken DelPontee and his last bodyguard into custody. Brandeis had gotten out of the car when the shooting stopped and was running toward her daughter. When they saw each other, Gabrielle begged Anderson to put her down. Mother and daughter embraced in a tearful reunion. Anderson picked her up again and they all walked to the ambulance.

Nathan was sitting in the street holding a very weak CaSandra in his arms. There were tears on his cheek. He had removed his cap and was looking down at her.

"You little fool," he said softly pushing her hair back from her face. "Why did you do that?"

She looked up at him. Shutting her eyes against the burning pain from the wound, she tried to smile. She reached up, straining and touched his cheek with her finger where his dimple would show.

"Because I love you," she sobbed. "I've **always** loved **you**, Nathan. You just wouldn't give me a play." Her eyes clouded and she coughed. "You had to be loyal to your friend always, huh Nate? You just wouldn't..." She closed her eyes.

Nate pulled her closer and did not let her go until the paramedics arrived to put her in the first ambulance. The paramedics in the second ambulance treated Gabrielle's feet and tended to the wounded men before transporting them to the hospital.

Even though Jimmy was handcuffed, he was permitted to ride with his mother to the hospital. An officer accompanied him. Anderson, Gabrielle and Skeeter followed in the Pathfinder. They offered to take Brandeis but she declined.

After most of the people had left the scene except for a handful of police who were milling around gathering evidence, Brandeis went over to Nathan. He was still sitting in the street. There was blood on his hands. She used the damp towel she had gotten from the paramedics to wipe his hands. Since he was sitting down, she could easily put her arms around his neck. Nathan took advantage of the comfort she offered. He allowed himself to release some of the pain he had been holding for years since the day he found out that CaSandra had aborted his baby. He wept bitterly.

CHAPTER XIX

Anderson pulled into Temple University Hospital's parking lot within fifteen minutes of the ambulance. They found Jimmy in a waiting area outside of intensive care. He was pacing back and forth. His handcuffs had been removed but there was a police officer close by. The two brothers came face to face in silence. They stood looking at each other for a long moment sharing an unspoken grief. Jimmy was the first to turn away. Gabrielle and Skeeter observed from the doorway. Anderson reached out and touched Jimmy's shoulder. He was sure Jimmy would lash out at him or pull away. The younger man stiffened for a second and then Anderson felt his brother's shoulders drop as Jimmy lowered his head. A doctor walked up to them and told Jimmy to go in and see his mother. Jimmy left the room immediately.

When Nathan and Brandeis arrived, Anderson was talking to the doctor. Everyone was standing close enough to see the grave expression on the doctor's face.

"How is she?" Anderson asked anxiously.

"Are you family?" the doctor asked.

"I'm her other son," Anderson told him realizing that this was one of the few times he had said it out loud.

"We've done all we can. There was a lot of internal damage and she's lost a great deal of blood," the doctor said carefully. "It's really just a matter of time now. I'm so sorry." The doctor walked away. A gloomy silence hovered in the room.

Jimmy returned, looking haggard. His eyes were red. His usual arrogance was gone. He looked like someone who had aged ten years in two hours. The usual swagger to his walk was missing when he went over to Nathan. He wiped the perspiration from his forehead and swallowed the lump in his throat.

"My mom wants to see you," he said simply.

Nathan looked confused. "But what about An...?"

"Not yet." Jimmy interrupted. "She asked for **you**." Nathan hurried toward the room.

Jimmy walked over to Gabrielle who was standing next to Skeeter.

"I'm sorry." It was all he could manage. He sounded defeated, like a man who had lost all strength of will. A tear was rolling down Gabrielle's face. Jimmy reached up and touched it with his finger. He looked at Skeeter. He pressed his lips together tightly for a minute. "Thanks," he said in a choked voice. "I know you made Mom happy when you two were together," his voice cracked. He inhaled deeply, stifling his tears. He threw his shoulders back and walked over to the police officer. He looked back at everyone one more time and tried to force a courageous smile.

"Okay, we're outta here!" he said thrusting his arms out in front of him. The policeman handcuffed his hands behind him and escorted him from the room. Brandeis and Gabrielle held on to each other, occasionally wiping one another's tears. Skeeter was leaning against the wall. Anderson stood waiting and watching the door to CaSandra's room.

Moments later, Nathan opened the door and motioned for Anderson to come. Anderson walked quickly but the closer he got to CaSandra room, the more his feet began to feel like lead. He had never been this close to his mother. He felt the bed give under his weight. He sat gingerly, trying not to add to her discomfort. He reached to touch her hand and was surprised when she squeezed his with weak pressure. They looked at each other for what seemed like a long while. CaSandra's breathing was long and labored. Each time she struggled, the hole in Anderson's heart grew deeper.

"You look good," she said hoarsely with a half-smile. "I sure make pretty babies." She tried to reach up to touch his face. Anderson took her hand and put it to his cheek.

He couldn't speak. He had so many questions but he could not say a word. He turned to look at Nathan who was standing at the foot of the bed. Nathan moved his gaze from Anderson to CaSandra. His face was troubled and hurt. When CaSandra averted her eyes to him, his face grew stern.

"Tell him," his voice was firm, demanding obedience. With those two words he turned on his heels and left.

When Anderson looked back at his mother, he saw tears. He took a tissue from the nightstand and wiped her face. She turned her face and kissed his hand. The gesture surprised him and frustration tore at him. He wanted to hold his mother. He wanted his mother to hold him.

"So many questions right?" CaSandra replied hoarsely. Anderson nodded.

"Air, that's what he calls you right?" CaSandra said softly, "don't be angry with Nate. Anything he didn't tell you was because I swore him to secrecy. I made him promise not to tell you too much about me. I was afraid that once you found out how I messed up my life, you'd hate me."

Anderson tried to protest but when CaSandra moaned from the pain, Anderson decided to let her finish.

"He's a good man," she continued looking toward the door then back at Anderson, "and your dad was a good man too. He didn't deserve what I did to him but I just didn't love Clayton in high school or even after. The truth is, I was in love with Nate, the whole time but he wouldn't talk to me…except on your father's behalf. I wanted Nate so-o bad. I even thought that if I dated your father, I could make him jealous. I was hoping Nate would finally care about me."

She grimaced and waited for the pain to subside. She gripped his hand until the pain stopped. Anderson's other hand trembled as he touched her face again.

"But your godfather, he was a stubborn man. He sure kept his distance from me. So, I decided that if I couldn't have him, I'd have his friend. Why not? Clay already loved me and I

175

knew it. Besides, it's not as if I didn't like your dad. Not very nice, huh? Well, that's your mom. That's how I was back then."

Anderson shook his head and CaSandra smiled before she continued.

"It's funny, in high school, we were like the three musketeers. We went almost everywhere together. Nathan tried to keep his distance but a lot of times, I insisted that he come along. Your dad, not realizing that something was up, even accused him of being rude when he tried to avoid us. But Nate? Oh, he knew what I was doing. He wanted no parts of it." CaSandra tried to laugh and wheezed instead.

Anderson placed his palm firmly against her chest until she calmed down.

"Oh Air," she sighed, "when I realized I was pregnant with you, I panicked. I didn't know what to do. I knew I couldn't have you because I didn't love your father. I didn't want to trap him. I confided in Nate thinking I could get him to care. But no-o. He was furious with me. So, I ran away but not far enough away. Nate brought me back. I finally agreed to give you to your father. Your dad was hurt. He made me promise not to see you unless I was ready and willing to be a real mother. Later, when I heard about Clay's death, I came to the funeral but I felt so stupid. I couldn't bring myself to see you. I had made such a mess of everything."

Anderson took a washcloth from the nightstand. He moistened it with water from the pitcher and dabbed his mother's face. CaSandra blinked her eyes and gave a feeble smile.

"Once you grew up, I saw how successful you'd become and decided against being part of your life," she continued. "You were doing so well; I didn't want you to have a mother you'd be ashamed of."

"But Mom," Anderson protested, "what you did earlier in your life wouldn't have made a difference. All I ever wanted was to know you; to spend time with my mother."

"That's what Nate said whenever he tracked me down but your grandfather didn't agree. The times I found enough nerve to call, he wouldn't let me talk to you. I can't say I blamed him." She coughed and tried to shift her position. Anderson helped her as much as he could without hurting her. "I can't blame anybody really. I said some pretty harsh things about dark-skinned people trying to reinforce a prejudice I didn't really believe myself." She gave a half smile.

"I mean, I was trying to put distance between me and my friends because of a career I wanted. There I was saying all this stuff about dark-skinned people while some of the people who treated me the best, who loved me…who cared for me were…" She swallowed and tears steamed down the sides of her face again.

"I fell on hard times too. One time Nate found me, I was pretty strung out. I had already had Jimmy. Nate discovered us in a dingy apartment in South Jersey. Jimmy was starving, dirty and I was a mess. Nate cleaned us up. He helped me go "cold turkey" and in return I seduced him." CaSandra sobbed and tried to turn her face into the pillow. Anderson gripped her hand as another sharp pain overtook her.

"I thought he loved me then. I thought I'd finally won because he'd given in to me. Turns out that it was only because I caught him when he was most vulnerable. The one woman he ever loved left him for another man. He was devastated. I'd never seen him so broken. He reached for me in a moment of weakness and I loved him so much, I took what I could get. When I found out I was pregnant and he still didn't want me, I fell apart." Her voice wavered for a minute and a tear slid down her face.

"That's when you had the abortion?" Anderson spoke gently.

"You have been doing your homework," she injected. Anderson nodded.

"It was Nate's only baby. He's never forgiven me for that. He was injured on his job shortly after…he can't have any more children. I robbed him of his chance to be a father, except that when Clayton died he became devoted to you." She patted his hand. "He had a hard time forgiving Jason until recently."

"Jason?" Anderson arched an eyebrow questioningly. "You mean Jason Duvall?"

CaSandra tried to nod her head and she started to cough.

"Poor Jason, he was so pitiful. He was one of my biggest fans. He would turn up almost every place I did a fashion show. We became friends and we even dated sometimes but he wanted more than that. I tried my old scheme again. I tried to use Jason to make Nate jealous and I took it too far. It was worse than with your father. There were so many lies." She sucked in several short breaths. Before she could speak, CaSandra shed some quiet tears.

"Once I realized I was pregnant and since Nate wouldn't have anything to do with me, I tricked Jason. I got him drunk and well, you can fill in the rest." CaSandra squeezed her son's hand and tried to smile. "I'm not proud of my life and I didn't think you would be either."

"Back then, I kept hoping Nate would come around before I had to tell him about the baby. But your godfather still wouldn't see me the way I wanted him to. Eventually, I had to tell Jason the truth; that he was not the father of the baby. Then I confessed to him who I really cared about. I thought I was letting him down easy. By the time I made up my mind about the pregnancy, I was fourteen weeks along. Depressed. I told Jason what I wanted to do and he paid for my abortion. Nate got wind of it afterwards and went ballistic. He felt that with all his money, Jason should have paid for a decent operation. He probably would have but only if I had agreed to move in with him. He still wanted me after what I'd done to him but I couldn't do it. Later, when I got clean again, I owed it to Jimmy to try to be a good mother especially since I failed you and after what I did to Nate." CaSandra's breathing was labored and Anderson tried to quiet her but she just had to get it all out.

"You know what's worse? Nate didn't realize it was his baby until I ended up in the hospital. I had thoroughly convinced him it was Jason's. He knew something was up when Jason was so willing to pay for the abortion. Poor Jason tried to make up for what he did by bidding a lot of money for the portrait. You know the one? Lonely Woman." Anderson nodded. CaSandra moaned softly. As much as it hurt to keep talking, she had to try.

"I kept track of you though. When you started your own business, I was so proud. Then I heard you were looking for me. That's when I got paranoid."

"Who sent me the pictures and the other information?" Anderson asked shifting his weight on the bed.

"I did. I mean, I had Skeeter send it for me. We're kinda close. Isn't that a laugh? He's around your age, I think." she tried to chuckle. Her voice dropped lower. "He's kept me posted on some of your cases. If I had information that could help you, I gave it to Skee." She took a long, deep breath. It came out ragged and she coughed again. Her eyelids began to droop.

"Mom!" Anderson called anxiously.

"I'm just tired, Son," It was the first time she had called him that—*Son*. Anderson closed his eyes as if trying to replay the sound of it over and over. He was afraid he would never hear it again. "I knew this case meant a lot to you and I wanted to help." She sighed again. Another pain overwhelmed her.

"Mom?" Anderson interrupted her, "did you know my middle name is Isaac?" He needed to tell her that. He needed for her to know it now. Wanted her to know that his father had loved her enough to forgive her for leaving their son.

Even though it hurt to do it, she grabbed his hand with both of hers. "Isaac? That's my name backwards, kind of—your father had this thing about finding out what names were backwards. He called me Cassi. Clay would go on and on about our future. He said when we had a baby he would...Oh God." Fresh tears streamed down her face as she tried to smile.

"I know, Mom. Dad wanted me to have something from you. He always loved you. I love you too, Mom. I don't hate you for—for anything. You did what you thought you had to do."

This time, Anderson did reach down and hug his mother. Their partial embrace was with aching tenderness. Anderson's strong hands eased around her shoulders, gently against the pillows. Mother and son had tears in their eyes. His mother motioned him closer. She eased his hand up to her neck. Anderson looked into her eyes and knew she wanted him to remove her necklace. She was wearing a black opal on a chain. He looked at her in surprise and she smiled as he unhooked it.

"This is my birthstone," he almost whispered. His eyes were shining.

"I know," his mother said softly. Her strength was fading. "You've always been close to me. You keep it now. Give it to…" she coughed.

"Gabrielle." Anderson offered as he touched her hand. He took both of her hands in his and looked at his mother. The pain was unbearable. He had just found her and he was losing her.

"Do what you can for Jimmy, Isaac, but don't try to get him off. We all have to pay for what we do. Your father used to say that so often." She wheezed, then closed her eyes against the pain. When she opened them, mother and son looked at each other for a long, agonizing moment. Anderson nodded and he felt his mother's hands go limp in his own. He leaned down and kissed her forehead. She was weak but she struggled to hold on and ask one more favor.

"Could you help me say a prayer and then send Skeeter in, please? I need to talk to him." Her voice was weak, fading.

"But Mom," he knew what she was doing but he didn't want to leave her.

"Please, Son," her voice scratched when she begged. Anderson choked back another rush of raw emotions. He hated to hear her beg. They said a prayer together as he held her hand.

CHAPTER XX

Gabrielle and Skeeter were the only ones in the waiting room when Anderson returned. Gabrielle noticed the sadness in his eyes immediately. She went to him. He took her hand and walked over to Skeeter. The young man was still leaning against the wall. His hands were jammed into his pockets; his head hung low to hide the naked pain tearing at his heart.

"My mom is asking for you," he told Skeeter as he touched his shoulder. Skeeter ran to her room without hesitation.

Anderson and Gabrielle sat down. It was a somber moment that no words could change so they sat quietly holding hands.

Skeeter's visit with CaSandra lasted about fifteen minutes. When he re-entered the waiting area, his head cast down. Anderson jumped up and rushed toward him. Skeeter bit the inside of his jaw against the other pain in his gut. Anderson saw the look on Skeeter's face and noticed that his eyes were red. He tried to push past his friend. Skeeter grabbed Anderson by the shoulders. Since Anderson was the bigger man, Skeeter had to use his body weight to subdue his determined friend.

"No, Air, please." He said firmly. Then with the next ragged breath, "She's gone." He felt Anderson's shoulders droop against his hands. He put a supportive arm around his friend. Skeeter inhaled long and slow and bit his tongue to suppress the tears that were brimming in his eyes.

"Air, she didn't want you to see her when..." he didn't finish. He just blinked and shook his head.

They walked back to where Gabrielle was sitting and Anderson sat down in the chair next to her. He pressed thumb and index finger at the bridge of his nose to ward off a headache. So much happened and so fast. He was trying to take it all in, especially the part about his mother helping him to crack the investigation. She must have known it would be dangerous. She **had to** know the consequences might be fatal, even for her.

Anderson was quiet for a good while. Gabrielle reached for his hand. He looked at her and then at Skeeter who was leaning against the wall. He could tell by the way Skeeter's shoulders were moving that his friend was taking CaSandra's death hard. He had no idea that this man had loved his mother. Anderson was grateful that she had had someone who genuinely cared about her and had not abused her. *Life is so ironic, one chapter was opening and another was closing in the span of a few hours.*

Not letting go of Gabrielle's hand, Anderson stood up. Gabrielle walked with him as he took the few steps that closed the gap between him and Skeeter. Anderson put his hand on Skeeter's shoulder and Skeeter raised his pain-stained eyes to the ceiling as he fought for composure. Gabrielle reached out with her other hand and gave his a slight squeeze. Skeeter looked at her and forced a grateful half-smile.

"Come on, I'll give you a ride back to your car," Anderson told him.

After pausing at the nurses' station to leave his business card and inform the nurse that he would be back soon, Anderson exited the hospital with his friends. As they rode back to Twenty-second and Allegheny, the only sound in the car was a soft jazz instrumental on the radio. Anderson pulled up next to Skeeter's car. Skeeter exited from the rear passenger seat.

"Air, You can - uh, give me a call in a few days if you need anything—or if there's anything else you want to know about...about your mom...or whatever," Skeeter's voice was raw with grief. He was leaning on the car window when he spoke. He wanted to say something else but nothing came. He and Anderson shook hands. Anderson held on for a few seconds longer when Skeeter tried to pull away. Skeeter felt a pain for his friend grab at his chest and he tightened his grip for a moment. No words were spoken. No words were needed. They just looked at each other with new understanding; that from this point on their friendship would be much deeper.

"Thanks Wendell," Anderson replied solemnly. Gabrielle gasped as she looked up in surprise. Anderson had only used this man's proper name twice since he'd met him. This was the second time.

Skeeter put the index finger of his other hand to his lips in a cautioning gesture. "Sh-h-h" He looked around pretending to be concerned that someone might learn his true identity. He managed a slight smile. They did one of the usual Black man's handshakes and Skeeter went to get in his car. A few moments later, his steel-gray '72 Jaguar went tearing down the street with music by Hiroshima bouncing off his windows.

Anderson did not pull off right after Skeeter left. He seemed to suddenly be plagued by indecision. He sat there gripping the steering wheel—tight. He unfastened his seat belt. He did not know what he wanted to do. Finally, he turned to look at Gabrielle. He took her hand and touched the back of it to his face. Gabrielle moved as close to him as her seat belt would allow. She rested her head on his shoulder and he held her. He held her for a while without speaking. As a result of all that happened, their friendship was far from casual. She would be vital to him now. He'd lost his mother. The mother he never really knew. He'd lost his brother. The brother he never knew he had. Even though he could probably visit him in prison, Anderson doubted if Jimmy would even want to see him. His father had been killed when he was a young boy and his grandfather had died a year ago. Who did he have left?

"Do you know where Nate went?" Anderson asked when he could finally speak.

When he returned to the waiting area from his mother's room, he noticed that Nathan and Brandeis were gone. There had been so much going on and he was so overwhelmed, he was just now asking about his godfather. Gabrielle nodded as she looked up at him. She squeezed his hand.

"One of mom's neighbors had agreed to watch the house since the door was broken. He paged Nathan a while ago because he had to leave. Nathan and Momma left when you went in to be with your mother." Her voice faded on the last part of her sentence.

"Oh Gigi. There is so much I don't understand."

"What do you mean?" Gabrielle was looking at him now with tender concern in her eyes that tore at his heart. *Why couldn't we have met under much calmer circumstances? But if we had, would we be this drawn together?* These were questions that raced through Anderson's mind as he held her. These along with some other pressing matters.

"It appears that the whole time I was searching for my mom, Nate knew where she was. He knew and he didn't tell me. Why would he do that? Why would he keep that from me? My mom explained some of it but Nate knew how important this was." There was a tinge of anger in his voice that made Gabrielle shiver in his arms.

"Air," she began softly looking up at him, "the only way to clear this up is to talk to him. You need to go to him and let him explain. He would not deliberately hurt you, Nathan loves you. If he kept this information from you, I'm sure there's a good reason. Give him the chance to tell you what it is. Let's go to my mom's so the two of you can clear this up. You have to do it now, tonight."

"You're amazing—you know that?" For the first time this night he smiled at her.

"I got skills," she said, imitating Nate, "but don't tell my mother." Anderson chuckled.

Letting her settle back in her seat, Anderson shifted himself back behind the wheel and refastened his seat belt. He turned the key in the ignition. A few minutes later, as he drove toward Mt. Airy Circle, Anderson popped a cassette in the player on the dashboard. Gabrielle was surprised that he had decided not to play one of his CD's. A pensive look came over her face as she listened to an instrumental version of "Everything Must

Change." When she realized that Anderson was humming the melody, she smiled. *It's going to be all right*, she thought.

Nathan had repaired Brandeis's door and they were sitting on the living room sofa talking over cups of hot tea. Brandeis had put on a videotape but neither of them was really watching the screen.

"I knew he was upset with me the minute he met me on stakeout," Nathan told her.

"We didn't get a chance to hash it out before everything went crazy."

"You can't possibly believe that he doesn't want you in his life anymore. You've treated him like a son. He loves you." Brandeis tried to sound encouraging. "Why would he stop now?"

"Because I lied to him, Brandy," Nathan answered in a voice laced with frustration and worry. "I knew how much he wanted to find his mother. When I think about what this search was doing to him, how the false leads would tear him apart—I...I had vital information and I deliberately kept it from him. I couldn't take it anymore. This whole situation was like a thorn in our friendship and I had to do something."

"What did you do?" Brandeis asked because she knew he needed to talk.

"I slipped an envelope in Cassi's folder on the off chance that he'd recheck it but even that wasn't a guarantee. Cassi...she begged me over and over not to tell Air where she was. But the closer we got to DelPontee, I knew it was unavoidable. Now, he'll probably never speak to me again, let alone forgive me."

"Just like a typical father; you're deciding for me again. Why don't you let **me** speak for myself?" Anderson broke in from the hallway. He kept his face void of expression so Nathan was not sure what to think. He and Gabrielle had heard everything from the hallway as they entered the house. Once he realized how his godfather was agonizing over the whole situation, he decided that a confrontation was not necessary. Driving to Brandeis's house, Anderson had some time to think about all the things his mother had told him. He realized just how much Nathan loved his entire family. He squeezed Gabrielle's hand and smiled which assured her that they would be all right.

Gabrielle waved her door keys as she looked at her mother. No one had heard them when they entered the house. Brandeis went to her daughter and hugged her. Then she tugged Anderson's shirtsleeve like a little child would do. When he leaned toward her she gave him a hug and a pat on the back.

"I think you two have some unfinished business but if the two of you decide to go wrestling around, please, don't break anything." She was teasing and Anderson smiled. Still, he was grateful for the moment's pause. His face remained unreadable. Mother and daughter tipped off to the kitchen to allow the men some privacy.

Nathan rose from the sofa as Anderson walked toward him. The two men stood face to face for a moment. Nathan looked worried. Anderson still wore no expression at all. He did that to keep Nate on edge for a few seconds. He held out his hand, the way he often did to greet someone he was meeting for the first time.

Nathan looked at Anderson's face and then down at his extended hand. He took it to mean that their relationship had changed to something more formal—much more distant. A slap across the face would have had the same impact on his emotions. Reluctantly, he accepted Anderson's hand for the handshake. *This is better than nothing,* he thought. *Sometimes, you take what you can get.* Nathan resolved in that moment to win back his godson's trust no matter how long it took.

When Anderson felt the weak grip of Nathan's hand, he realized that his long-time friend had misinterpreted his actions. Nathan relaxed his hand after the handshake but Anderson, remembering a martial arts move, grabbed Nathan by the wrist. He pulled his uncle-godfather-partner-mentor-friend toward him and hugged him the way a son would hug his long, lost father. Nathan was caught completely off guard. His first reaction was to go into defense mode. Then, he returned Anderson's bear hug with relief and enthusiasm. They tightened their grip on each other for one very long moment.

"You let me decide what I can or cannot forgive," Anderson scolded near Nathan's ear as he embraced the older man. "You have been a big part of my life for a whole lot of years. That will never change. Do you hear me?...Never change." He spoke emphatically as he gave Nathan a few slaps on the back.

When they stepped back from each other their faces were equally wet with tears. They both wiped them away with the back of their hands.

"I'm not saying I fully understand everything you did but someone reminded me that you had to have a good reason. When you're ready to talk we'll talk." He was smiling at Nathan who was still composing himself. "They also reminded me that you've always had my back, no matter what." Anderson glanced toward the doorway as he spoke and Nathan immediately understood that the someone had to be Gabrielle.

"Uncle Nate," Anderson's voice was raspy and he had not used that term of endearment in years, "you've always been a good and loyal friend. I'm just discovering how much of a friend you have been to my **whole** family; for that, I'll always be grateful. As a matter of fact, you're all the family I have now." Anderson's voice was filled with anguish as he re-acknowledged his loss but he refused any new tears. Nate was touched by the reference Anderson had used. He hadn't heard it for a long time.

"Of course, now—" Anderson was saying, "you'll have to step aside just a little." Anderson paused when Gabrielle and Brandeis walked back into the room. He was smiling as he held out his hand to Gabrielle. When she went to him, he put his arm around her shoulder. He looked at her with tender affection and smiled. They both looked at Nathan.

Nathan smiled a broad, deep-dimpled smile as Brandeis approached him. She handed him and Anderson tissues and then she took Nathan's hand.

"Son," Nathan had not referred to him that way using a serious tone in a while. It felt right at this moment. "I doubt that **that** will be a problem." Everyone was wiping tear-stained faces but smiling at the same time.

EPILOGUE

Brandeis and Nathan decided to take their empty teacups into the kitchen where they could sit and make plans for the Fourth of July cookout. As soon as Anderson and Gabrielle were alone, he hugged her tight and buried his face in her neck. Gabrielle heard him growl playfully and she giggled. She stepped back so she could look into his eyes. Then, on tiptoes, she kissed him very gently on the lips. Anderson could not conceal the look of surprise that shone from his eyes.

"What was that for?" He asked smiling.

"For you," she said smiling back, "I see good things in the future and they're all for you."

ABOUT THE AUTHOR

"EBONIA"- for some a pseudonym might seem passé but RuNett Nia Ebo likes using it because writing fiction takes her into another "zone" far away from the normal. Until recently, Nia has only been known for her poetry and titles like *Dish-Rag Love, We Be A Nation* and the world renowned *Lord, Why Did You Make Me Black?* were her main sources of notoriety. Although this is her first fiction romance, she is already working on the second.

Miss Ebo loves seasonal employment. She works as a Tax Consultant in the winter, Creative Writing Instructor in the summer and an Outreach Worker, Motivational Speaker and Public Relations Coordinator the rest of the year. She is a very busy community activist in Philadelphia where she lives close to her five sons and four grandchildren. She loves God and gives Him all credit for her writing talent.

This author can be contacted at her website.

www.Ebo-Nia.net or email her poetebo@blackplanet.com